# Anxiety Hacks

# Books By The Author

30 DAYS PLANT-BASED DIET FOR AGING

Train Your Brain: Mindfulness Meditation For Anxiety, Depression, ADD, and PTSD ii

# Anxiety Hacks

Effective Methods, Tools, and Tips for Rapid

Anxiety Relief

**Dr Evelyn James O.K**

# Copyright Information

iv

# Table of Contents

v

# Acknowledgments

First and foremost, I would like to convey my heartfelt appreciation to my family, whose continuous support and encouragement made this book possible. Your love, compassion, and belief in me have been my greatest source of strength.

A special thank you to my great friend Stephen. Your insight, kindness, and direction have been crucial along this journey. Your support has had a lasting influence on this work and my life.

Thank you all for being my pillars of strength and inspiration.

# Introduction

Anxiety is a prevalent issue influencing millions of individuals globally. Despite its commonality, many individuals struggle to find effective ways to manage and surmount it. This book, **"Anxiety Hacks: Effective Methods, Tools, and Tips for Rapid Anxiety Relief,"** seeks to provide readers with a comprehensive guide to comprehending anxiety and equipping them with practical tools to alleviate it. Whether you're looking for immediate relief from an anxiety attack, pursuing natural remedies, or striving to eliminate anxiety from your life altogether, this book offers valuable insights and strategies to help you achieve your goals.

The primary purpose of this book is to empower you with knowledge and techniques to manage anxiety effectively. By examining various aspects of anxiety, including its psychological and physiological components, and understanding how different factors such as diet, lifestyle, and medications influence it, you will be better prepared to address your anxiety holistically. This book is not a substitute for professional medical advice, but it can be a valuable complement to professional treatment, offering practical ideas and methods that you can integrate into your daily life.

Anxiety can be debilitating, impeding your ability to function in routine situations. However, with the proper tools and knowledge, it is possible to regain control over your life. This book is designed to be a comprehensive resource, covering a broad spectrum of topics related to anxiety. From immediate relief techniques to long-term management strategies, dietary interventions, and comprehending the effects of drugs on anxiety, this book seeks to be your go-to guide for managing anxiety.

## Understanding Anxiety: A Brief Overview

Before delving into the various methods and techniques for managing anxiety, it's necessary to have a fundamental understanding of what anxiety is. Anxiety is a natural stress response and can be beneficial in some situations. It can alert us to perils and help us remain focused and motivated. However, when anxiety becomes excessive or persistent, it can interfere with our daily lives and become a disorder.

Anxiety disorders are the most prevalent mental health disorders in the world, affecting millions of individuals of all ages. They can appear in various ways, including generalized anxiety disorder (GAD), panic disorder, social anxiety disorder, and specific fears. Each variety of anxiety disorder has its unique characteristics, but they all share common features such as excessive concern, fear, and physical symptoms like a rapid heartbeat and shortness of breath.

The causes of anxiety disorders are diverse and numerous. They can include genetic factors, brain chemistry, personality, and life events. Understanding the fundamental causes of anxiety can help in devising effective treatment and management strategies. It's essential to recognize that anxiety is not a sign of weakness or a character defect, but rather a common and treatable condition.

In addition to its psychological impact, anxiety can also have significant physical effects. Chronic anxiety can contribute to various health problems, such as heart disease, digestive issues, and a compromised immune system. Therefore, addressing anxiety is not only crucial for mental health but also for comprehensive physical well-being.

## How to Use This Book

This book is structured to provide a comprehensive guide to managing anxiety, offering both immediate alleviation techniques and long-term management strategies. Here's how to make the most of this resource:

Read Through the Chapters Sequentially: The book is organized into chapters that build upon each other. Starting with a fundamental comprehension of anxiety, the book progresses to immediate relief techniques, long-term management strategies, dietary interventions, alternative therapies, the impacts of drugs, community support, preventive measures, and coping with triggers. Reading the chapters in order will give you a thorough comprehension of anxiety and equip you with a broad range of tools to manage it.

Refer to Specific Sections as Needed: While perusing the book sequentially is recommended, you can also use it as a reference guide. If you are experiencing an anxiety attack and need immediate relief, you can go directly to the chapter on immediate anxiety relief techniques. If you're interested in dietary adjustments to manage anxiety, you can jump to the chapter on dietary interventions.

Apply the Techniques and Strategies: The book offers practical techniques and strategies that you can integrate into your daily existence. As you read through the chapters, attempt to implement the methods that resonate with you. Experiment with different methods to find out what works best for you. Remember that managing anxiety is a personal endeavor, and what works for one person may not work for another.

Keep an Open Mind: Anxiety management is not a one-size-fits-all approach. This book covers a wide spectrum of techniques, from traditional methods to alternative therapies. Keep an open mind and be willing to attempt different approaches. What may seem unconventional at first might turn out to be highly effective for you.

Seek Professional Help When Needed: This book is a valuable resource for managing anxiety, but it is not a substitute for professional medical advice or treatment. If your anxiety is severe or persistent, it is essential to seek assistance from a mental health professional. They can provide personalized treatment plans and support to help you manage your anxiety effectively.

By understanding anxiety and implementing the methods and strategies outlined in this book, you can take control of your anxiety and lead a healthier, more fulfilling existence. Remember, managing anxiety is a journey, and it's acceptable to take it one step at a time. This book is here to guide you along the path, providing you with the tools and knowledge you need to overcome anxiety and achieve enduring relief.

# Chapter 1: Understanding Anxiety

## 1.1 What is Anxiety?

Anxiety is a universal human experience, a psychological and physiological condition that functions as a natural response to perceived threats or stressors. Emotions of stress, worried thoughts, and bodily changes including elevated blood pressure characterize it. While anxiety can be beneficial in brief bursts—enhancing alertness and performance—it becomes problematic when it is excessive, persistent, and interferes with daily life. This section attempts to comprehensively comprehend anxiety, detailing its definition, various types, common symptoms, and signs.

### Definition and Types of Anxiety Disorders

Anxiety, at its root, is a multifaceted condition that encompasses a variety of mental health disorders. It is essential to distinguish between everyday anxiety and anxiety disorders. Everyday anxiety is a normal aspect of existence. It is a response to specific situations, such as taking a test or making an essential decision. This form of anxiety is temporary and generally subsides once the distressing event has passed. In contrast, anxiety disorders are more severe, and persistent, and can occur without an apparent catalyst. They represent a group of related conditions, each with its unique features, but all characterized by excessive fear and anxiety.

**Generalized Anxiety Disorder (GAD)**

Generalized Anxiety Disorder (GAD) is among the most common anxiety disorders. It involves chronic anxiety, exaggerated concern, and tension, even when there is little or nothing to provoke it. People with GAD find it difficult to regulate their anxiety and often anticipate disaster. They may fret excessively about health, money, family, work, or other issues. This fretting often feels uncontrollable and can dominate a person's thoughts to the extent that it interferes with daily functioning.

**Panic Disorder**

Panic Disorder is characterized by recurrent, unanticipated panic attacks—sudden periods of intense dread that may include palpitations, sweating, trembling, shortness of breath, and a sense of impending catastrophe. These attacks can occur without warning and can be exceedingly debilitating. Individuals with Panic Disorder often live in dread of the next attack, which can lead to significant lifestyle changes to avoid potential triggers.

**Social Anxiety Disorder**

Social Anxiety Disorder, also known as social phobia, entails an intense dread of social or performance situations in which embarrassment may occur. Individuals with this disorder have a fear of being judged, disgraced, or humiliated by others. This anxiety can be so severe that it interferes with daily activities such as speaking in meetings, attending social gatherings, or even dining in front of others.

**Specific Phobias**

Specific Phobias are characterized by an intense dread of a specific object or situation, such as heights, flight, or spiders. The dread is typically out of proportion to the actual danger posed by the object or situation and can lead to avoidance behavior. Encountering or even ruminating about the phobic stimulus can induce significant anxiety.

## Obsessive-Compulsive Disorder (OCD)

Obsessive-Compulsive Disorder (OCD) entails unwanted, persistent impulses (obsessions) and repetitive behaviors (compulsions). Individuals with OCD feel compelled to perform these behaviors in response to their obsessions or according to rigorous standards. Compulsive behaviors are intended to reduce anxiety or prevent a feared event or situation, but they provide only transient relief and are not connected realistically to what they are meant to neutralize or prevent.

## Post-Traumatic Stress Disorder (PTSD)

Post-Traumatic Stress Disorder (PTSD) can develop after exposure to a traumatic event, such as a natural disaster, severe accident, terrorist act, war/combat, or rape. Individuals with PTSD may experience intrusive thoughts, nightmares, and recollections of the traumatic event, leading to severe anxiety. They may also avoid situations that remind them of the trauma and experience heightened reactions such as increased irritability or difficulty sleeping.

## Common Symptoms and Signs

Understanding the symptoms and signs of anxiety is crucial for early detection and effective management. While the symptoms can vary depending on the specific anxiety disorder, there are commonalities across different varieties.

**Emotional Symptoms**

- Excessive fretting: One of the hallmark symptoms of anxiety is excessive fretting. This concern is often disproportionate to the actual situation and can dominate a person's thoughts.
- Irritability: Anxiety can lead to heightened irritability, often as a result of the persistent state of tension and anxiety.
- Restlessness: Individuals with anxiety often feel on edge or restless, as if they cannot unwind or find serenity.
- Anticipatory Anxiety: This involves fretting about future events or prospective outcomes, often leading to avoidance behaviors.

**Physical Symptoms**

- Increased pulse Rate: Anxiety can cause the pulse to accelerate, leading to palpitations that can be quite distressing.
- Muscle Tension: Chronic anxiety often leads to muscle tension, particularly in the neck, shoulders, and back.
- perspiration: Excessive perspiration, particularly in social or stressful situations, is a common symptom.
- Trembling or Shaking: Anxiety can cause perceptible trembling or shaking, particularly during panic attacks.
- Shortness of Breath: Many people with anxiety experience shortness of breath or a sensation of being unable to recover their breath.
- Gastrointestinal Issues: Anxiety can manifest in physical symptoms such as stomachaches, vertigo, or digestive issues.

**Cognitive Symptoms**

- Racing Thoughts: Anxiety often leads to a rapid, overwhelming deluge of thoughts that can be difficult to control.
- Difficulty Concentrating: The preoccupation with anxiety and dread can make it hard to focus on tasks or remember information.
- Catastrophic Thinking: This involves envisioning the worst-case scenario and feeling persuaded that it will happen, often without realistic evidence.

**Behavioral Symptoms**

- Avoidance: Avoiding situations, locations, or people that provoke anxiety is a common behavioral symptom. This avoidance can significantly impact one's quality of life and daily functioning.
- Compulsive Behaviors: In the case of OCD, individuals may engage in repetitive behaviors or rituals to reduce anxiety, even if they are aware that these behaviors are irrational.
- Social Withdrawal: People with social anxiety may disengage from social interactions to prevent potential embarrassment or judgment.

Recognizing these symptoms and signs is the first step towards obtaining assistance and managing anxiety effectively. It is crucial to note that anxiety disorders are treatable, and many people find relief through a combination of therapy, medication, lifestyle adjustments, and self-help strategies. If you or someone you know is struggling with anxiety, it is essential to seek professional assistance to investigate the best treatment options.

## 1.2  The Mental Condition of Anxiety

Understanding the mental condition of anxiety is crucial for comprehending how it manifests and affects an individual's existence. Anxiety is not merely a transient state of concern or fear but a complex psychological phenomenon that involves various cognitive processes and affective responses. In this section, we will investigate the psychological aspects of anxiety and examine the cognitive patterns and distortions that perpetuate this condition.

## Psychological Aspects

Anxiety is firmly entrenched in our psychological framework. It is influenced by a combination of genetic predispositions, early life experiences, and individual personality traits. The psychological aspects of anxiety comprise emotional responses, coping mechanisms, and behavioral tendencies that are often engrained over time.

### Emotional Responses

At the core of anxiety resides a set of emotional responses that can be acute and overwhelming. These emotions are often disproportionate to the actual situation and can persist long after the initial stimulus has passed. Common physiological responses include:

- Fear: Fear is a fundamental emotion in anxiety. It is an adaptive response that prepares the body to confront or avoid peril. However, in anxiety disorders, panic becomes excessive and persistent, often in the absence of actual threat.

- Apprehension: This entails a sense of dread or anxiety about future events. Individuals with anxiety often foresee negative outcomes, leading to chronic concern and tension.
- Helplessness: Feeling out of control or unable to manage the anxiety can lead to a profound sense of helplessness. This can exacerbate the emotional turmoil and make it difficult to find effective coping strategies.

**Coping Mechanisms**

People with anxiety often develop specific coping mechanisms, some of which can be maladaptive. Understanding these mechanisms is essential for developing healthier methods to manage anxiety.

- Avoidance: Avoidance is a common coping strategy where individuals steer clear of situations or activities that provoke anxiety. While avoidance provides transient respite, it reinforces anxiety over time and limits one's ability to function fully.
- Safety Behaviors: These are actions performed to prevent anticipated outcomes. For example, someone with social anxiety might avoid eye contact or remain mute in a group to avoid judgment. While these behaviors can reduce anxiety in the present, they prevent the individual from confronting and overcoming their concerns.

- Rituals and Compulsions: In conditions like Obsessive-Compulsive Disorder (OCD), rituals and compulsions are used to regulate anxiety. These behaviors, such as repeated checking or washing, provide transient respite but can become time-consuming and disruptive.

**Behavioral Tendencies**

Behavioral tendencies in anxiety are often characterized by hypervigilance, restlessness, and difficulty in unwinding. These behaviors are a direct response to the emotional and cognitive aspects of anxiety and can significantly impact daily functioning.

- Hypervigilance: This is an enhanced state of sensory sensitivity and an exaggerated intensity of behaviors whose purpose is to detect hazards. Hypervigilance can lead to exhaustion and difficulty concentrating on non-threatening tasks.
- Restlessness: Persistent anxiety can make it challenging to unwind or remain still. This restlessness can interfere with sleep and overall well-being.
- Avoidance Behavior: Avoidance of feared situations or activities can lead to significant lifestyle adjustments and isolation, further perpetuating the cycle of anxiety.

# Cognitive Patterns and Distortions

Cognitive patterns and distortions play a prominent role in the perpetuation of anxiety. These are biased methods of reasoning that reinforce negative emotions and maladaptive behaviors. Identifying and resolving these cognitive distortions is a critical component of cognitive-behavioral therapy (CBT), a widely used approach in the treatment of anxiety disorders.

**Catastrophizing**

Catastrophizing involves envisioning the worst-case scenario and believing it to be inevitable. This cognitive distortion amplifies anxiety by focusing on prospective calamities rather than realistic outcomes.

 Example: A person may believe, "If I make a mistake during this presentation, everyone will think I'm incompetent, and I'll lose my job."

**Overgeneralization**

Overgeneralization is the tendency to view a single negative event as a never-ending pattern of defeat. This pattern of thinking can lead to a sense of hopelessness and increased anxiety.

Example: After failing one exam, a student might conclude, "I always fail tests; I'll never succeed in school."

## Mind Reading

Mind reading involves presuming that others are thinking negatively about you without any actual evidence. This distortion can foster social anxiety and hinder interpersonal relationships.

Example: Someone might assume, "I can tell they think I'm awkward and boring," without any actual indication that this is true.

## Fortune Telling

Fortune telling is the belief that you can foretell future events, often presuming negative outcomes. This can lead to anticipatory anxiety and avoidance behaviors.

Example: "I'm going to embarrass myself at the party, so I might as well not go."

## All-or-Nothing Thinking

All-or-nothing thinking, also known as black-and-white thinking, entails seeing situations in extremes without recognizing the intermediate ground. This can create unrealistic expectations and increased anxiety when those expectations are not met.

Example: "If I'm not perfect, I'm a total failure."

## Emotional Reasoning

Emotional reasoning is the process of presuming that your negative emotions reflect the truth about a situation. This distortion can make it difficult to challenge apprehensive thoughts.

Example: "I am terrified of flying; thus, it must be dangerous."

## Should Statements

Should statements entail rigid guidelines about how you or others should conduct? These statements can create a sense of failure and remorse, contributing to anxiety.

Example: "I should always be serene and collected. If I'm apprehensive, I'm feeble."

## Personalization

Personalization is the tendency to blame yourself for events outside your control, leading to feelings of remorse and increased anxiety.

Example: "My buddy didn't react to my message; it must be because I said something wrong."

## Labeling

Labeling involves designating a fixed, negative label to yourself or others based on a singular event or behavior. This can lead to self-defeating beliefs and behaviors.

Example: "I made a mistake; I'm such a failure."

Addressing these cognitive distortions involves recognizing them when they occur, challenging irrational thoughts, and replacing them with more balanced and realistic ones. Cognitive-behavioral techniques, such as cognitive restructuring and mindfulness, are effective instruments for modifying these patterns and reducing anxiety.

## 1.3 The Physical Condition of Anxiety

Anxiety, while fundamentally a mental health condition, has profound physical manifestations that can affect almost every system of the body. Understanding these physiological responses and their impacts on physical health is crucial for comprehending the full scope of anxiety and for developing effective strategies for its management. This section delves into the physiological responses associated with anxiety and analyzes how chronic anxiety can impact overall physical health.

# Physiological Responses

When anxiety strikes, the body reacts in a way that prepares it to confront potential hazards, a reaction known as the "fight-or-flight" response. This response is an evolutionary mechanism designed to enhance our chances of survival in hazardous situations. However, in modern times, this response can be provoked by non-life-threatening stressors, leading to various physiological changes.

## Activation of the Sympathetic Nervous System

The sympathetic nervous system (SNS) serves a central function in the body's response to anxiety. When the brain perceives a threat, it signals the adrenal glands to release stress hormones, including adrenaline and cortisol. These hormones induce several physiological changes:

- Increased pulse Rate and Blood Pressure: Adrenaline causes the pulse to beat quicker and blood vessels to constrict, increasing blood pressure. This ensures that more oxygen and nutrients are delivered to muscles, priming the body for fast action.
- Rapid respiration: To supply more oxygen to the body, respiration becomes quicker and shallower. This can contribute to sensations of shortness of breath and dizziness.

- Muscle Tension: Muscles tense to prepare for action. Chronic anxiety can contribute to persistent muscle tension, causing pain and distress, particularly in the neck, shoulders, and back.
- Sweating: The body increases perspiration production to calm itself down during intense physical activity. This can result in clammy palms and excessive perspiration, even in mild conditions.

**Digestive System Reactions**

The digestive system is very responsive to stress and anxiety. When the fight-or-flight response is activated, the body diverts energy away from non-essential functions like digestion to prioritize immediate survival demands. This can lead to various gastrointestinal symptoms:

- Nausea and Stomach Pain: Anxiety can cause the stomach to produce excess acid, leading to nausea, stomach pain, and discomfort.
- Diarrhea or Constipation: The pace at which food travels through the digestive system can be altered, resulting in either diarrhea or constipation.
- Irritable defecation Syndrome (IBS): Chronic anxiety is a known catalyst for IBS, a condition characterized by abdominal pain, cramping, and changes in defecation behaviors.

## Cardiovascular System Responses

The cardiovascular system is significantly impacted by anxiety. The constant discharge of stress hormones can have long-term effects on heart health:

- Palpitations: Anxiety can produce the sensation of a racing or pounding pulse, known as palpitations. These can be distressing and contribute to further anxiety.
- Hypertension: Chronic anxiety can contribute to sustained elevated blood pressure, increasing the risk of cardiovascular diseases such as heart attacks and strokes.

## Respiratory System Responses

The respiratory system's response to anxiety is often immediate and noticeable:

- Hyperventilation: Rapid, shallow breathing, or hyperventilation, is a common response to anxiety. This can lead to lightheadedness, sensations in the extremities, and even syncope.
- Asthma Exacerbation: Anxiety can induce or worsen asthma symptoms, leading to shortness of breath and chest constriction.

## Endocrine System Responses

The endocrine system, which regulates hormone production, is also affected by anxiety:

Cortisol Release: Chronic anxiety leads to the prolonged release of cortisol, the primary stress hormone. Elevated cortisol levels over time can impair the immune system, increase blood sugar levels, and contribute to weight gain and metabolic disorders.

## Impact on Physical Health

The physiological responses to anxiety, particularly when they become chronic, can have significant impacts on physical health. Understanding these impacts is essential for appreciating the complete burden of anxiety and the significance of addressing it comprehensively.

**Cardiovascular Health**

Chronic anxiety is a risk factor for several cardiovascular conditions:

- Heart Disease: Persistent high blood pressure and elevated stress hormone levels can damage blood vessels, increasing the risk of coronary artery disease and heart attacks.
- Arrhythmias: Anxiety can cause irregular heartbeats, or arrhythmias, which can be uncomfortable and, in some cases, hazardous.

## Gastrointestinal Health

The digestive system's response to chronic anxiety can contribute to long-term issues:

- Gastritis and Ulcers: Excessive gastric acid secretion can cause inflammation of the stomach lining (gastritis) and increase the risk of developing ulcers.
- Chronic Digestive Disorders: Conditions such as IBS can become chronic, substantially affecting quality of life through persistent pain, inflammation, and bowel irregularities.

## Respiratory Health

Anxiety's impact on the respiratory system can exacerbate existing conditions and contribute to new ones:

- Chronic Obstructive Pulmonary Disease (COPD): Anxiety can exacerbate symptoms in individuals with COPD, making respiration more difficult and reducing overall lung function.
- Frequent Respiratory Infections: Stress can impair the immune system, making the body more susceptible to respiratory infections such as colds and pneumonia.

## Musculoskeletal Health

Chronic muscle tension and discomfort are common in individuals with anxiety:

- Chronic Pain Conditions: Persistent muscle tension can lead to conditions such as tension headaches, migraines, and chronic back pain.
- Fibromyalgia: Anxiety is often associated with fibromyalgia, a condition characterized by pervasive musculoskeletal pain and fatigue.
- 

**Immune System Health**

The immune system's function can be compromised by chronic anxiety:

Reduced Immunity: Prolonged stress hormone release can impair the immune system, reducing the body's ability to fend off infections and increasing susceptibility to illnesses.

Inflammation: Chronic anxiety can contribute to increased inflammation in the body, which is linked to various chronic diseases, including autoimmune disorders and diabetes.

**Overall Well-being**

The cumulative effects of protracted anxiety on physical health can substantially impact overall well-being and quality of life:

- Sleep Disturbances: Anxiety can interfere with sleep, resulting in insomnia or poor-quality sleep. This, in turn, can exacerbate anxiety and other health issues.
- Fatigue: The constant state of tension and alertness associated with anxiety can contribute to persistent fatigue and exhaustion, making daily activities more challenging.
- Lifestyle Changes: Chronic anxiety can contribute to significant lifestyle changes, such as reduced physical activity, poor nutrition, and social withdrawal, all of which can negatively impact physical health.

Understanding the physiological responses and physical health impacts of anxiety underscores the importance of a holistic approach to its management. Addressing anxiety involves not only psychological interventions but also lifestyle adjustments and medical remedies to mitigate its wide-ranging effects on the body.

# Chapter 2: Immediate Anxiety Relief Techniques

In instances of acute anxiety, finding immediate alleviation is crucial for regaining control and composure. Anxiety can escalate rapidly, causing overwhelming physical and emotional responses that can feel debilitating. This chapter provides practical, effective techniques to reduce anxiety immediately, concentrating on breathing exercises and grounding techniques. These methods can be implemented anywhere, at any time, providing a fast pathway to serenity and stability.

## 2.1 How to Reduce Anxiety Immediately

### Breathing Exercises

Breathing exercises are one of the most effective methods for managing acute anxiety. They work by stimulating the parasympathetic nervous system, which promotes relaxation and counteracts the body's fight-or-flight response. By focusing on controlled, deliberate respiration, you can reduce physical symptoms of anxiety such as accelerated heart rate, shallow breathing, and muscle tension.

## Deep Breathing

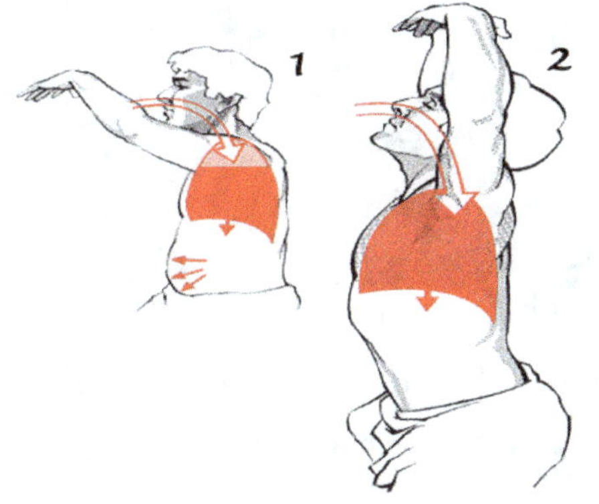

Deep breathing, also known as diaphragmatic breathing or abdominal breathing, is a simple yet potent technique to calm the nervous system. Here's how to practice through breathing:

- Find a Comfortable Position: Sit or recline down in a comfortable position. Ensure your back is erect, and your shoulders are relaxed.
- Place Your Hands: Place one hand on your sternum and the other on your abdomen.
- Inhale Slowly: Take a slow, deep breath in through your nostrils, allowing your abdomen to expand as you fill your lungs with oxygen. Your thorax should remain relatively still.
- Hold the Breath: Now hold your breath for a count of four.
- Exhale Slowly: Exhale slowly and thoroughly through your mouth, feeling your abdomen contract as you release the oxygen.
- Repeat: Repeat this procedure for 5-10 minutes, focusing on the rise and fall of your abdomen and the rhythm of your respiration.

## 4-7-8 Breathing

The 4-7-8 breathing technique, devised by Dr. Andrew Weil, is another effective method for immediate anxiety relief. It helps regulate respiration and promote a sense of tranquility. Follow these steps:

- Prepare: Sit or lie down in a comfortable position, with your back erect and your shoulders relaxed.
- Inhale: Inhale silently through your nostril for a count of four.
- Hold: Hold your breath for a count of seven.
- Exhale: Exhale completely and audibly through your mouth for a count of eight.
- Repeat: Repeat the cycle at least four times, progressively increasing to eight cycles as you become more accustomed to the technique.

**Box Breathing**

Box breathing, also known as square breathing, is a technique used by Navy SEALs to remain composed and focused under duress. It entails equal intervals of inhaling, holding, exhaling, and holding again. Here's how to practice box breathing:

- Position Yourself: Sit or stand in a comfortable position with your back erect and your shoulders relaxed.
- Inhale: Inhale steadily through your nostril for a count of four.
- Hold: Now hold your breath for a count of four.
- Exhale: Exhale steadily through your mouth for a count of four.
- Hold Again: Hold your breath again for a count of four.
- Repeat: Continue this pattern for several minutes, focusing on preserving a constant, rhythmic respiration.

## Grounding Techniques

Grounding techniques are designed to bring your focus back to the present moment, helping to distract your mind from apprehensive thoughts and reduce the intensity of an anxiety attack. These techniques use the senses—sight, hearing, touch, taste, and smell—to reconnect with the immediate environment.

**The 5-4-3-2-1 Technique**

The 5-4-3-2-1 grounding technique is a basic yet effective method for soothing the mind during an anxiety attack. It involves identifying objects around you using your senses. Here's how to perform it:

- Find Your Surroundings: Sit or stand in a comfortable position and take a long inhalation.
- Identify Five Things You Can See: Look around and name five things you can see. This could be anything in your environment, such as a timepiece on the wall, a plant, or a novel.
- Identify Four Things You Can Touch: Focus on four objects you can handle. This could be the texture of your attire, the feel of your chair, or the coldness of a glass of water.
- Identify Three Things You Can Hear: Listen and identify three sounds you can hear. This might be the murmur of a computer, birds tweeting outside, or distant traffic.

- Identify Two objects You Can scent: Take note of two objects you can scent. If you're at home, this might be the fragrance of cooking or a nearby candle.
- Identify One Object You Can Taste: Focus on one object you can taste. This could be the residual flavor of a meal or simply observing the taste of your saliva.

**Grounding Through Physical Sensation**

Using physical sensations to ground yourself can be particularly effective during intense anxiety. Here are a few methods to try:

- Cold Water Splash: Splash cold water on your face or apply a cold compress to your forehead. The sensation can startle you into the present moment and reduce the intensity of an anxiety attack.
- Texture Exploration: Keep a small object with a distinct texture, like a polished stone or a piece of fabric, in your pocket. When you feel apprehensive, focus on the texture of the object, noting its feel, temperature, and any patterns or irregularities.
- Progressive Muscle Relaxation: This technique involves tensing and then gently releasing each muscle group in your body. Start with your fingertips and work your way up to your cranium. Tense each muscle group for about five seconds and then release for fifteen seconds, noticing the contrast between tension and relaxation.

**Grounding Through Visualization**

- Visualization can help create a mental retreat from anxiety by focusing on a tranquil scene or situation. Here's how to practice grounding through visualization:

- Find a calm Space: Sit or recline down in a comfortable, calm place where you won't be disturbed.

- Close Your Eyes: Close your eyes and take a few slow breaths to unwind.

- Imagine a Calming Scene: Visualize a place where you feel secure and relaxed. This could be a shore, a forest, a cozy room, or any place that offers you calm.

- Engage Your Senses: In your consciousness, engage all your senses in this calming scene. Notice the colors, the sounds, the scents, and the sensations. Imagine the warmth of the sun on your skin, the sound of waves colliding, or the scent of pine trees.

- Stay Present in the Scene: Spend a few minutes immersed in this visualization, enabling yourself to feel tranquil and relaxed.

## 2.2 Ways to Calm an Anxiety Attack

Experiencing an anxiety attack can be immensely distressing, characterized by overwhelming panic, rapid heartbeat, shortness of breath, and a sense of losing control. In these instances, having effective techniques to calm yourself is crucial. This section provides a step-by-step guide and emergency coping strategies to help you manage and ameliorate the symptoms of an anxiety attack promptly and effectively.

## Step-by-Step Guide

Managing an anxiety attack involves a series of deliberate actions designed to soothe the mind and body. Follow this step-by-step guide to regain control during an anxiety attack:

**Step 1: Recognize the Signs**

The first step in managing an anxiety attack is to recognize that you are experiencing one. Common indications include a racing pulse, rapid respiration, sweating, trembling, chest discomfort, dizziness, and a sense of impending catastrophe. Acknowledge these symptoms as an anxiety attack rather than a more severe medical issue, like a heart attack.

**Step 2: Find a Safe Space**

If possible, move to a location where you feel safe and secure. This could be a quiet room, a secluded area in a public place, or even a location where you can sit down and collect your thoughts.

**Step 3: Focus on Your Breathing**

Breathing exercises are fundamental in calming the body's physiological response to anxiety. Use the deep breathing technique described earlier:

- Inhale steadily through your nose, filling your lungs and expanding your abdomen.
- Just hold your breath for a count of four.
- Exhale steadily through your mouth, sensing the tension released from your body.
- Repeat this process for several minutes, focusing solely on your respiration and its rhythm.

**Step 4: Practice Grounding Techniques**

Grounding techniques can help divert your attention from anxiety symptoms to your immediate environment. The 5-4-3-2-1 technique is particularly effective:

- Identify 5 objects you can see.
- Identify 4 objects you can handle.
- Identify 3 objects you can perceive.
- Identify 2 items you can scent.

- Identify 1 item you can sense.

**Step 5: Use Positive Affirmations**

Positive affirmations can help counteract negative thoughts and reassure yourself during an anxiety attack. Repeat tranquil phrases such as:

- "I am safe."
- "This will pass."
- "I am in control."
- "I can handle this."

**Step 6: Engage in Light Physical Activity**

If practicable, engage in a gentle physical activity like walking, stretching, or even shaking out your palms. Physical movement can help reduce the excess epinephrine in your system and promote a sense of serenity.

**Step 7: Use Distraction Techniques**

Distracting your mind from apprehensive thoughts can be very beneficial. Engage in an activity that requires your concentration, such as reading, listening to music, or doing a puzzle. These activities can help redirect your focus away from anxiety.

**Step 8: Seek Support**

If you are secure, reach out to someone you trust. Talking to a companion, family member, or therapist can provide solace and reassurance. Sometimes, just hearing a calming voice can make a significant difference.

## Emergency Coping Strategies

In addition to the step-by-step guide, having a set of emergency coping strategies can be invaluable during an anxiety attack. These strategies are designed to be fast, effective, and simple to implement in any situation.

### Use a Stress Ball or Fidget Device

Keeping a stress ball or fidget device on board can provide a tactile distraction during an anxiety attack. Squeezing a stress ball or using a fidget spinner can help relieve tension and focus your mind on a simple, repetitive action.

### Cold Water Method

The sensation of chill can startle your system into a more present state. Splashing frigid water on your face or holding an ice compress against your forehead can help ground you and reduce the intensity of an anxiety attack.

**Visualize a Calm Place**

Visualization can be a potent tool to transport your mind away from the current anxiety-inducing situation. Close your eyes and imagine a place where you feel utterly at ease, such as a beach, a peaceful forest, or a comfortable room. Engage all your senses in this visualization, envisioning the sights, sounds, scents, and sensations of this calming place.

**Progressive Muscle Relaxation**

This technique involves systematically tensing and then relaxing each muscle group in your body, commencing from your toes and working your way up to your cranium. This process helps relieve physical tension and promotes overall relaxation.

**Mindfulness and Meditation Apps**

There are numerous applications available that offer guided meditations and mindfulness exercises specifically intended to help manage anxiety. Apps such as Calm, Headspace, and Insight Timer provide immediate access to soothing audio recordings and breathing exercises that can help soothe your mind during an anxiety attack.

**Counting Backwards**

Counting backward from 100 by sevens (100, 93, 86, etc.) requires concentration and can help divert your attention from apprehensive thoughts. This mental exercise can also help calm down hasty thinking and bring a sense of control.

**Aromatherapy**

Using essential oils such as lavender, chamomile, or peppermint can have a soothing effect. Inhale directly from the bottle, position a few drops on a cotton ball or use a diffuser to fill your space with a soothing fragrance.

**Writing It Down**

Journaling your thoughts and emotions can be an effective method to process and manage anxiety. Write down what you are experiencing, what provoked the anxiety, and any actions you can take to feel better. This act of writing can help organize your thoughts and provide a sense of release.

**Chewing Gum**

Chewing gum can help reduce anxiety by fostering rhythmic movement and sensory engagement. The act of chewing can distract your mind and provide a simple, repetitive action that is soothing.

## 2.3 Natural Ways to Relieve Anxiety Fast

In addition to traditional methods and immediate coping strategies, natural remedies can provide effective and holistic relief from anxiety. This section examines herbal remedies and aromatherapy as natural approaches to alleviate anxiety rapidly. These methods utilize the power of nature to promote relaxation and calm, offering accessible and mild options for managing anxiety.

### Herbal Remedies

Herbal remedies have been used for centuries to treat numerous maladies, including anxiety. Certain herbs possess properties that can help soothe the mind, reduce tension, and promote a sense of well-being. Here are some of the most effective herbal remedies for anxiety relief:

### 1. Valerian Root

Valerian root is renowned for its soothing and sedative properties. It has been used traditionally to alleviate insomnia and anxiety. Valerian root works by increasing the levels of gamma-aminobutyric acid (GABA) in the brain, which serves to reduce neural activity and promote relaxation.

**How to Use:** Valerian root can be consumed as a tea, tincture, or capsule. To create valerian tea, steep one teaspoon of desiccated valerian root in boiling water for 10-15 minutes. Drink it 30 minutes to an hour before nighttime or during periods of acute anxiety.

### 2. Passionflower

Passionflower is another herb known for its anxiolytic properties. It is notably effective in reducing symptoms of generalized anxiety disorder (GAD) and can help with insomnia and nervous restlessness.

**How to Use:** Passionflower can be consumed as a tea, tincture, or capsule. For tea, steep one teaspoon of desiccated passionflower in heated water for 10-15 minutes. Drink it up to three times daily, as required.

### 3. Lavender

Lavender is widely recognized for its tranquil fragrance and is often used in aromatherapy. Lavender can also be ingested to help alleviate anxiety symptoms. Studies have shown that

lavender can reduce anxiety, enhance mood, and promote improved sleep.

**How to Use:** Lavender can be consumed as a tea, essential oil, or capsule. To create lavender tea, steep one to two teaspoons of desiccated lavender blossoms in hot water for 10 minutes. Lavender essential oil can be diffused or applied topically after dilution with a carrier oil. For capsules, follow the dosage instructions on the product label.

### 4. Chamomile

Chamomile is a soothing herb that is well-known for its tranquil and anti-inflammatory properties. It is notably effective in reducing mild to moderate anxiety and enhancing sleep quality.

**How to Use:** Chamomile is commonly consumed as a tea. Steep one to two tablespoons of dried chamomile flowers in lukewarm water for 5-10 minutes. Drink it up to three times daily, particularly before bedtime for improved sleep.

### 5. Ashwagandha

Ashwagandha is an adaptogenic herb that helps the body adapt to stress and reduces anxiety. It works by modulating the body's stress response and lowering cortisol levels, thereby promoting a sense of calm and well-being.

**How to Use:** Ashwagandha can be consumed as a granule, capsule, or tincture. For the powder form, combine one teaspoon into a smoothie, tepid milk, or water. Follow the dosage instructions on the product label for capsules or tinctures.

## Aromatherapy

Aromatherapy entails the use of essential oils extracted from botanicals to promote physical and psychological well-being. Inhaling the fragrance of essential oils can have a profound influence on mood and anxiety levels. Here are some of the most effective essential oils for anxiety relief:

**1. Lavender Oil**

Lavender oil is one of the most well-known and versatile essential oils for anxiety relief. Its calming scent helps to reduce tension and anxiety and promotes restful slumber.

**How to Use:** Add a few droplets of lavender oil to a diffuser or vaporizer. You can also add a few droplets to a tepid bath or apply it topically after diluting with carrier oil, such as coconut or jojoba oil.

## 2. Bergamot Oil

Bergamot oil has elevating and calming properties that make it effective for reducing anxiety and enhancing mood. It is often used in aromatherapy to relieve tension and promote relaxation.

**How to Use:** Add a few droplets of bergamot oil to a diffuser or inhale it directly from the bottle. You can also combine it with carrier oil and apply it to your wrists or temples.

## 3. Frankincense Oil

Frankincense oil is known for its grounding and soothing properties. It helps to calm down breathing and promote a sense of inner serenity, making it useful for managing anxiety.

**How to Use:** Use a diffuser to disperse frankincense oil in the air or add a few droplets to a tepid bath. You can also combine it with a carrier oil and apply it to the back of your neck or the soles of your feet.

## 4. Ylang Ylang Oil

Ylang-ylang oil has a pleasant, floral fragrance that is both uplifting and tranquil. It serves to reduce stress and anxiety and can enhance mood.

**How to Use:** Add a few droplets of ylang-ylang oil to a diffuser or inhale it directly from the vial. It can also be diluted with a carrier oil and applied to the skin or added to a bath.

## 5. Chamomile Oil

Chamomile oil, like the herb itself, has comforting and tranquil properties. It serves to reduce anxiety, promote relaxation, and enhance sleep quality.

**How to Use:** Diffuse chamomile oil in your living space or add a few droplets to a tepid bath. You can also dilute it with a carrier oil and apply it to your skin, particularly the wrists and temples.

## Blending Essential Oils

Blending essential oils can enhance their individual effects and create a personalized aromatherapy experience. Here are a couple of mixtures specifically designed to assuage anxiety:

Calming Blend: Combine 3 drops of lavender oil, 2 drops of frankincense oil, and 2 drops of bergamot oil. Use in a diffuser or combine with a carrier oil for topical application.

Relaxation Blend: Mix 3 drops of chamomile oil, 2 drops of ylang-ylang oil, and 2 drops of lavender oil. Use in a diffuser or add to a tepid bath for a tranquil experience.

## Safety Considerations

When using herbal remedies and essential oils, it is crucial to consider safety and potential interactions:

- Consult a Healthcare Professional: Before commencing any new herbal remedy, particularly if you are taking other medications or have underlying health conditions, consult with a healthcare professional.

- Quality Matters: Use high-quality, unadulterated essential oils and herbal products from reputable sources to ensure their safety and effectiveness.
- Patch Test: When using essential oils topically, always perform a patch test first to check for any skin sensitivity or allergic reactions.

# Chapter 3: Long-term Anxiety Management

Effectively managing anxiety is not just about finding immediate respite during episodes of acute stress; it's also about employing long-term strategies that address the core causes of anxiety and promote overall mental well-being. By making sustained lifestyle adjustments and cultivating consistent habits, it is possible to substantially reduce the impact of anxiety and, for many, eliminate it. This chapter concentrates on how to get rid of anxiety forever through transformative lifestyle adjustments and the development of consistent habits that support mental health.

## 3.1 How to Get Rid of Anxiety Forever

### Lifestyle Changes

Long-term anxiety management often begins with a comprehensive evaluation and modification of lifestyle choices. These modifications address various aspects of daily life, including physical health, emotional well-being, and environmental factors. Here are some important lifestyle adjustments that can help eliminate anxiety:

## 1. Regular Physical Activity

Exercise is one of the most effective natural methods to combat anxiety. Regular physical activity helps to reduce levels of the body's stress hormones, such as adrenaline and cortisol, while concurrently promoting the production of endorphins, compounds in the brain that act as natural painkillers and mood elevators.

- Types of Exercise: Incorporate a blend of aerobic exercises (like walking, running, and swimming) and strength training into your routine. Activities such as yoga and tai chi are also beneficial as they incorporate physical movement with mindfulness practices.
- Consistency: Now aim for at least 30 minutes of moderate activity most days of the week. Consistency is essential to reaping the long-term benefits of physical activity on mental health.

## 2. Balanced Diet

Nutrition plays a crucial influence on mental health. A balanced diet can help stabilize mood and energy levels, supplying the nutrients required for optimal brain function.

- Nutrient-rich foods: Focus on consuming a variety of fruits, vegetables, whole cereals, lean proteins, and healthy fats. Foods rich in omega-3 fatty acids, such as salmon and flaxseeds, are notably advantageous for brain health.
- Avoiding Triggers: Reduce or eliminate the intake of caffeine, sugar, and refined foods, which can exacerbate anxiety symptoms. Alcohol and recreational substances should also be used with caution, as they can interfere with anxiety management.

## 3. Quality Sleep

Adequate and restorative sleep is fundamental to mental health. Anxiety and sleep are closely associated; poor sleep can exacerbate anxiety, and anxiety can interfere with sleep.

- Sleep Hygiene: Establish a regular sleep schedule by going to bed and rising at the same time each day. Create a calming twilight routine, limit exposure to electronics before bed, and ensure your sleeping environment is comfortable and conducive to rest.
- Addressing Sleep Disorders: If you experience chronic sleep issues, consult a healthcare professional. Conditions such as insomnia or sleep apnea may require targeted interventions.

## 4. Stress Management Techniques

Learning to manage tension effectively is crucial for long-term anxiety management. Chronic stress is a significant contributor to anxiety, so developing strategies to manage stress is essential.

- Mindfulness and Meditation: Regular mindfulness practice and meditation can help reduce tension and enhance emotional regulation. Techniques such as deep breathing, gradual muscular relaxation, and guided visualization can be integrated into everyday routines.
- Time Management: Effective time management can help reduce the tension associated with work and personal responsibilities. Prioritize tasks, set realistic objectives, and take regular pauses to prevent burnout.

**5. Social Connections**

Strong social connections are vital for mental health. Positive relationships provide emotional support, reduce feelings of isolation, and offer opportunities for meaningful interactions.

- developing Relationships: Invest time in developing and maintaining relationships with family, colleagues, and community members. Join social clubs or organizations that reflect your interests and ideals.
- Seeking Support: Don't hesitate to seek support from loved ones when required. Talking about your feelings and experiences can provide relief and cultivate a sense of connection.

## Consistent Habits for Mental Well-being

In addition to lifestyle adjustments, cultivating consistent routines that promote mental well-being is essential for managing anxiety in the long term. These practices should become part of your daily regimen, creating a stable foundation for emotional resilience.

### 1. Regular Practice of Relaxation Techniques

Incorporating relaxation techniques into your daily routine can help manage anxiety and tension levels. Practices such as yoga, tai chi, and qigong combine physical movement with mental focus, promoting relaxation and emotional balance.

Daily Routine: Set aside time each day for relaxation practices. Even a few minutes of deep breathing or mindfulness meditation can make a significant difference.

### 2. Journaling

Journaling is a potent instrument for processing emotions and reducing anxiety. Writing down your thoughts and sentiments can provide clarity, help identify patterns, and offer a sense of relief.

Daily Journaling: Make journaling a daily habit. Spend a few minutes each day writing about your experiences, emotions, and any insights you gain. This practice can help you monitor progress and identify triggers.

**3. Gratitude Practice**

Focusing on gratitude can alter your perspective and reduce anxiety. By routinely acknowledging the positive aspects of your life, you can cultivate a more optimistic outlook.

Gratitude Journal: Keep a gratitude journal where you write down three things you are thankful for each day. This practice can help cultivate a positive mindset and reduce tension.

**4. Engaging in Hobbies and Interests**

Engaging in activities you appreciate can provide a sense of accomplishment and purpose, reducing anxiety and enhancing overall well-being.

Regular Engagement: Dedicate time each week to pastimes and interests that bring you pleasure and fulfillment. Whether it's painting, gardening, reading, or playing a musical instrument, these activities can serve as a beneficial escape from tension.

**5. Continuous Learning and Growth**

Pursuing continuous learning and personal development can boost self-esteem and resilience, making it simpler to manage anxiety.

Lifelong Learning: Engage in activities that promote learning and personal development, such as taking courses, perusing books, or attending seminars. Setting and accomplishing personal objectives can provide a sense of purpose and accomplishment.

## 6. Professional Support

Regular check-ins with a mental health professional can provide ongoing support and guidance. Therapy can help you develop coping strategies, process emotions, and address underlying issues contributing to anxiety.

Therapeutic Relationship: Establish a regular schedule for therapy sessions, whether weekly, bi-weekly, or monthly, based on your requirements. A robust therapeutic relationship can provide a reliable source of support and insight.

## 7. Setting Boundaries

Learning to set and maintain healthy boundaries is crucial for protecting your mental well-being. Boundaries help manage tension, prevent burnout, and ensure that your requirements are met.

Clear Communication: Communicate your boundaries to others, and be consistent in enforcing them. This might entail saying no to additional responsibilities or taking time for yourself when required.

# 3.2 Cognitive Behavioral Techniques

Cognitive Behavioral Therapy (CBT) is one of the most effective evidence-based approaches for managing anxiety. It focuses on identifying and challenging negative thought patterns and beliefs while concurrently addressing the behaviors that contribute to anxiety. This section delves into the fundamental components of CBT: identifying and challenging negative beliefs and implementing behavioral interventions. By mastering these techniques, individuals can substantially reduce anxiety and enhance their overall mental health.

## Identifying and Challenging Negative Thoughts

Negative thought patterns, or cognitive distortions, are a hallmark of anxiety. These distorted methods of thinking perpetuate anxiety by reinforcing a cycle of dread and avoidance. The first step in cognitive-behavioral techniques is to identify these negative beliefs and challenge their validity.

### Identifying Negative Thoughts

Negative thoughts often occur automatically and can be difficult to recognize. However, with practice, individuals can learn to discern these thoughts and comprehend their impact on anxiety.

- Automatic Thoughts: These are spontaneous thoughts that arise in response to a situation. They are often negative and reflect sincerely held beliefs about oneself, others, or the world. For example, thinking "I will fail this presentation" before speaking in public.
- Thought Records: Keeping a thought record is a useful instrument for identifying negative beliefs. This involves writing down the situation that provoked the anxiety, the reflexive thoughts that arose, and the emotional response. Over time, this practice helps to highlight recurring negative thought patterns.

**Common Cognitive Distortions**

Understanding prevalent cognitive distortions can help individuals recognize and label their negative thoughts. Some of the most frequent distortions include:

- Catastrophizing: Expecting the worst conceivable outcome in any situation. For example, thinking "If I make a mistake, I will lose my job and never find another one."
- Overgeneralization: Drawing generalized, negative conclusions based on a singular event. For example, believing "I failed this test, so I am a failure at everything."
- All-or-Nothing Thinking: Seeing situations in black-and-white terms, without recognizing the intermediate ground.

For example, thinking "I am a horrible failure if I do not do this exactly.."

- Mind Reading: Assuming others are thinking negatively about you without any evidence. For example, "They must think I am ignorant since I made that mistake."

- Fortune Telling: Predicting negative future events without evidence. For example, "For instance, "I know this meeting will go absolutely horrible."."

**Challenging Negative Thoughts**

Once negative beliefs are identified, the next step is to challenge their veracity and validity. This involves investigating the evidence for and against the thought and developing more balanced, realistic perspectives.

- Examining the Evidence: Analyze the evidence that supports and contradicts the negative thought. For example, if you think "I always mess up," search for specific instances where you performed well to counter this belief.

- Alternative Perspectives: Consider alternative explanations and viewpoints. Ask yourself, "Is there another way to look at this situation?" For example, instead of thinking "I will fail," consider "I have prepared well, and I can do my best."

- Decatastrophizing: Question the likelihood and impact of the worst-case scenario. Ask yourself, "What is the worst that could happen, and how would I cope with it?" Often, the anticipated outcome is not as catastrophic as initially imagined.

- Realistic Statements: Replace negative notions with balanced, realistic statements. For example, alter "I can't handle this" to "This is challenging, but I have the skills and resources to manage it."

## Behavioral Interventions

Behavioral interventions in CBT focus on modifying the behaviors that contribute to and maintain anxiety. These interventions seek to disrupt the cycle of avoidance and promote adaptive coping strategies.

**Exposure Therapy**

Exposure therapy is a powerful behavioral intervention that involves progressively confronting feared situations or objects. The aim is to reduce avoidance behaviors and desensitize individuals to anxiety-provoking stimuli.

- Gradual Exposure: Create a hierarchy of feared situations, ranking them from least to most anxiety-provoking. Gradually expose yourself to these situations, commencing with the least worrisome and working your way up.

- Sustained Exposure: Remain in the anxiety-provoking situation until the anxiety decreases. This helps to demonstrate that the dread is manageable and that anxiety will diminish over time.
- Repeated Exposure: Consistent exposure is key to reducing anxiety. Repeat the exposure exercises routinely until the fear response decreases significantly.

**Behavioral Activation**

Behavioral activation involves increasing engagement in positive, gratifying activities to counteract the inactivity and withdrawal often associated with anxiety and depression.

- Activity Scheduling: Plan and timetable pleasurable and meaningful activities into your daily routine. This helps to counteract the tendency to withdraw and provides positive reinforcement.
- Goal Setting: Set small, achievable objectives to progressively increase your activity level. This can help develop confidence and motivation.

**Relaxation Techniques**

Incorporating relaxation techniques into daily routines can help manage the physiological symptoms of anxiety and promote overall well-being.

- Progressive Muscle Relaxation (PMR): This technique involves tensing and then relaxing each muscle group in the body. It serves to reduce muscle tension and promote physical relaxation.
- Deep Breathing Exercises: Practice deep breathing techniques to calm the nervous system and reduce physical symptoms of anxiety.
- Mindfulness Meditation: Being mindful is embracing the current moment without judgment. Regular mindfulness practice can reduce tension and enhance emotional regulation.

## Cognitive Restructuring

Cognitive restructuring is a process of identifying and challenging irrational or maladaptive thoughts and beliefs. It involves examining the evidence for these views, contemplating alternative interpretations, and developing more balanced perspectives.

- Thought Challenging: Identify irrational notions and challenge them with evidence-based reasoning. Change your negative ideas with more reasonable and optimistic ones.
- Positive Self-Talk: Try to develop a habit of positive self-talk. Encourage yourself with affirmations and supportive statements. For example, "I can handle this," or "I am capable and strong."

## Problem-Solving Skills

Developing effective problem-solving skills can help reduce anxiety by providing practical solutions to stressful situations.

- Identify the Problem: Clearly define the problem or challenge you are confronting.
- Generate Solutions: Brainstorm multiple prospective solutions. Don't censor your ideas at this juncture.
- Evaluate and Choose: Evaluate the pros and cons of each solution and choose the most practicable and effective one.
- Implement and Review: Implement the selected solution and review its efficacy. Adjust your approach if necessary.

**Cognitive-Behavioral Journaling**

Maintaining a CBT journal can help monitor your progress, identify patterns, and reinforce positive changes.

- Daily Entries: Record your thoughts, emotions, and behaviors daily. Consider their mutual effect.
- Progress Tracking: Note improvements and setbacks, and analyze what contributed to each. This serves to reinforce successful strategies and adjust ineffectual ones.

# Chapter 4:Dietary Interventions

The management of anxiety can be considerably influenced by nutrition, which plays a pivotal role in overall mental health. Research has demonstrated that certain foods and nutrients can alleviate anxiety symptoms by promoting brain function and regulating mood. In this section, the emphasis is on foods that alleviate anxiety rapidly, with a particular emphasis on nutrient-rich options. Additionally, an anti-anxiety diet plan is provided to foster long-term mental health.

## 4.1 Foods That Reduce Anxiety Fast

### Nutrient-rich Foods

Consuming a balanced diet rich in specific nutrients can help mitigate anxiety symptoms by optimizing brain health and regulating neurotransmitter function. Some of the most significant nutrients and their food sources that have been associated with decreased anxiety are as follows:

**1. Omega-3 Fatty Acids**

Brain health is contingent upon omega-3 fatty acids, specifically eicosapentaenoic acid (EPA) and docosahexaenoic acid (DHA). They have anti-inflammatory properties and play a crucial role in neurotransmitter function, which can help reduce anxiety.

**Sources:** Fatty fish (such as salmon, mackerel, and sardines), chia seeds, flaxseeds, hazelnuts, and algae-based supplements.

**2. Magnesium**

Magnesium is a mineral that helps modulate neurotransmitters and muscle function. It has a soothing effect on the nervous system and can help reduce symptoms of anxiety and tension.

**Sources:** Leafy green vegetables (such as spinach and kale), nuts and seeds (such as hazelnuts and pumpkin seeds), whole cereals (such as brown rice and quinoa), and legumes (such as black beans and lentils).

**3. B Vitamins**

B vitamins, particularly B6, B9 (folate), and B12, are vital for brain health and the production of neurotransmitters such as serotonin and dopamine, which influence mood and anxiety levels.

**Sources:** Whole grains, eggs, meat, fish, dairy products, verdant green vegetables, legumes, and fortified cereals.

## 4. Vitamin D

Vitamin D is crucial for overall brain health and has been linked to the regulation of mood and anxiety. Low levels of vitamin D are associated with an increased risk of anxiety and depression.

**Sources:** Sunlight exposure, fatty fish (such as salmon and mackerel), egg yolks, fortified dairy products, and supplements.

## 5. Zinc

Zinc is a trace mineral that plays a significant role in neurotransmitter function and the modulation of the brain's response to stress. Adequate zinc levels are essential for reducing apprehension.

**Sources:** Meat (notably beef and poultry), shellfish (such as oysters and crab), legumes, seeds, almonds, and dairy products.

## 6. Probiotics

Probiotics are beneficial microorganisms that support digestive health, which in turn influences brain health through the gut-brain axis. A healthy gut microbiome can help reduce anxiety and enhance mood.

**Sources:** Yogurt with live cultures, kefir, sauerkraut, kimchi, miso, tempeh, and other fermented foods.

## 7. Antioxidants

Antioxidants safeguard the brain from oxidative stress, which can exacerbate anxiety. Foods rich in antioxidants can help maintain optimal brain function and reduce anxiety symptoms.

**Sources:** Berries (such as blueberries, strawberries, and raspberries), dark chocolate, almonds, seeds, and colorful vegetables (such as bell peppers, beets, and spinach).

## Anti-Anxiety Diet Plan

Adopting an anti-anxiety diet involves incorporating nutrient-rich foods into your daily meals while avoiding foods that can provoke or exacerbate anxiety. Here is a comprehensive diet regimen developed to promote mental well-being and reduce anxiety:

**Breakfast**

**1. Omega-3 Smoothie**

**Ingredients:** 1 cup of spinach, 1 cup of frozen berries (blueberries or strawberries), 1 tablespoon of flaxseeds or chia seeds, 1 cup of unsweetened almond milk, and a teaspoon of plant-based protein powder (optional).

**Preparation:** Blend all ingredients until homogeneous. This smoothie is abundant in omega-3 fatty acids, antioxidants, and fiber, providing a nutritious start to the day.

## 2. Whole Grain Oatmeal

**Ingredients:** 1/2 cup of rolled oats, 1 cup of water or milk, 1 tablespoon of almond butter, and a fistful of fresh cherries.

**Preparation:** Cook the cereals in water or milk until tender. Stir in the almond butter and serve with fresh berries. This meal is abundant in fiber, B vitamins, and antioxidants.

## Lunch

### 1. Quinoa Salad

**Ingredients:** 1 cup of cooked quinoa, 1/2 cup of chickpeas, 1/2 cup of cherry tomatoes, 1/4 cup of diced cucumber, 1/4 cup of feta cheese, 2 teaspoons of olive oil, juice of 1 lemon, and a fistful of chopped fresh parsley.

**Preparation:** Combine all ingredients in a basin and stir well. This salad is filled with magnesium, protein, fiber, and healthful fats.

### 2. Grilled Salmon and Veggies

**Ingredients:** 1 salmon filet, 1 tablespoon of olive oil, 1 cup of broccoli florets, 1 cup of carrot segments, and a scattering of sesame seeds.

**Preparation:** Grill the salmon tenderloin with olive oil and simmer the vegetables. Sprinkle sesame seeds over the vegetables. This meal is abundant in omega-3 fatty acids, vitamins, and minerals.

**Snack**

### 1. Greek Yogurt with Nuts

**Ingredients:** 1 cup of Greek yogurt, 1 tablespoon of honey, and a fistful of assorted nuts (almonds, walnuts, and cashews).

**Preparation:** Mix the yogurt with honey and garnish with almonds. This snack provides probiotics, protein, and healthful lipids.

### 2. Hummus and Veggies

**Ingredients:** 1/2 cup of hummus and a variety of raw vegetables (carrot spears, cucumber segments, bell pepper sections).

**Preparation:** Serve the hummus with fresh vegetables for dipping. This refreshment is abundant in fiber, protein, and vitamins.

**Dinner**

## 1. Baked Chicken with Sweet Potatoes

**Ingredients:** 1 chicken breast, 1 tablespoon of olive oil, 1 sweet potato, 1 cup of steamed green beans, and a sprinkle of herbs (rosemary or thyme).

**Preparation:** Bake the chicken breast and sweet potato with olive oil and herbs. Serve with steaming green asparagus. This meal provides lean protein, fiber, and essential vitamins and minerals.

## 2. Lentil Soup

**Ingredients:** 1 cup of lentils, 1 minced onion, 2 cloves of garlic, 1 cup of diced tomatoes, 1 cup of shredded spinach, 1 tablespoon of olive oil, and 4 cups of vegetable broth.

**Preparation:** Sauté the onion and garlic in olive oil, add the lentils, tomatoes, and vegetable broth, and simmer until lentils are tender. Stir in the spinach before serving. This chowder is abundant in fiber, protein, and iron.

## Evening Snack

### 1. Dark Chocolate and Berries

**Ingredients:** 1 ounce of dark chocolate (at least 70% cocoa) and a fistful of fresh cherries.

**Preparation:** Enjoy the dark chocolate with berries as a delight. This refreshment provides antioxidants and a mood boost.

**2. Herbal Tea**

**Ingredients:** 1 cup of heated water, 1 chamomile tea bag, and a teaspoon of honey.

**Preparation:** Steep the chamomile tea leaf in boiling water for 5-10 minutes and add honey. Chamomile tea helps promote relaxation and enhance sleep quality.

## 4.2 Supplements and Vitamins

In addition to a well-balanced diet, certain supplements and micronutrients can play a crucial role in managing anxiety. While a healthy diet should always be the foundation of any wellness plan, supplements can provide additional support, particularly when it is challenging to obtain sufficient nutrients from food alone. This section examines the efficacy and safety of various supplements and vitamins known to assist in anxiety relief, along with their recommended dosages.

### Efficacy and Safety

**1. Omega-3 Fatty Acids**

Omega-3 fatty acids, notably EPA and DHA, are well-known for their anti-inflammatory properties and their function in brain health. Research has shown that omega-3 supplements can help reduce symptoms of anxiety and depression.

**Efficacy:** Studies suggest that omega-3 supplements can substantially reduce anxiety symptoms, particularly in individuals with generalized anxiety disorder (GAD). The anti-inflammatory effects and the enhancement of neurotransmitter function are believed to be the main mechanisms.

**Safety:** Omega-3 supplements are generally considered safe for most individuals. However, large dosages can contribute to adverse effects such as gastrointestinal upset, and excessive bleeding, particularly if taken with blood-thinning medications.

## 2. Magnesium

Magnesium is a vital mineral involved in over 300 biochemical reactions in the body, including those that regulate mood and stress response. Low levels of magnesium have been associated with increased apprehension.

**Efficacy:** Magnesium supplements have been shown to reduce anxiety, particularly in individuals with magnesium deficiency. It helps by modulating the activity of the hypothalamic-pituitary-adrenal (HPA) axis and enhancing the function of GABA, a neurotransmitter that promotes relaxation.

**Safety:** Magnesium supplements are generally safe when consumed at recommended dosages. High quantities can cause adverse effects such as diarrhea, nausea, and abdominal cramping.

People with kidney disease should consult a doctor before taking magnesium supplements.

## 3. Vitamins B

Vitamins B, particularly B6, B9 (folate), and B12, are essential for brain function and the production of neurotransmitters that regulate mood and anxiety.

**Efficacy:** B vitamin supplements can help mitigate anxiety symptoms by supporting the production of serotonin and dopamine. Deficiencies in these micronutrients are associated with increased anxiety and depression.

**Safety:** vitamins B are water-soluble, meaning they are generally safe, and excess quantities are excreted in urine. However, huge dosages can induce adverse effects such as nerve damage (B6) and skin rashes.

## 4. Vitamin D

Vitamin D is essential for overall health and has been linked to mood regulation and mental health. Low levels of vitamin D are related to an increased risk of anxiety and depression.

**Efficacy:** Supplementing with vitamin D can help enhance mood and reduce anxiety, notably in individuals with vitamin D deficiency. It serves a function in the synthesis of serotonin, a neurotransmitter involved in mood regulation.

**Safety:** Vitamin D supplements are generally safe when consumed within recommended limits. High quantities can lead to toxicity, resulting in hypercalcemia (excess calcium in the blood) and related health issues.

## 5. Zinc

Zinc is a trace mineral crucial for brain function and the modulation of the body's stress response. It is involved in the regulation of neurotransmitters and the maintenance of cognitive function.

**Efficacy:** Zinc supplementation has been shown to reduce anxiety symptoms, particularly in individuals with zinc deficiency. It supports the brain's response to stress and helps maintain balanced levels of GABA and glutamate.

**Safety:** Zinc supplements are safe when consumed at recommended dosages. Excessive ingestion can cause adverse effects such as nausea, vomiting, and copper deficiency.

## 6. Probiotics

Probiotics are beneficial microorganisms that support gastrointestinal health, which is closely linked to brain health through the gut-brain axis. A healthy gut microbiome can help reduce anxiety and enhance mood.

**Efficacy:** Probiotic supplements can help mitigate anxiety by reducing inflammation and producing neurotransmitters such as serotonin and gamma-aminobutyric acid (GABA). Studies have shown that specific strains, such as Lactobacillus and Bifidobacterium, are particularly effective.

**Safety:** Probiotics are generally secure for most individuals. However, individuals with compromised immune systems or severe maladies should consult a healthcare professional before use.

### 7. L-Theanine

L-Theanine is an amino acid present in tea leaves, particularly green tea. It is known for its soothing effects and ability to promote relaxation without causing lethargy.

**Efficacy:** L-theanine supplements can help reduce anxiety by increasing levels of GABA, dopamine, and serotonin. It also promotes alpha brain wave activity, which is associated with a state of relaxed alertness.

**Safety:** L-Theanine is generally considered safe with no significant adverse effects reported. It can be consumed alongside other supplements and medications without adverse interactions.

Recommended Dosages

While supplements can provide significant benefits, it is crucial to adhere to prescribed dosages to avoid potential adverse effects and interactions. Here are the general dosage guidelines for the supplements discussed:

**Omega-3 Fatty Acids:** A typical dosage ranges from 1,000 to 2,000 mg of combined EPA and DHA per day. It is advisable to choose high-quality fish oil supplements that are free from contaminants.

**Magnesium:** The recommended daily allowance (RDA) for magnesium is 400-420 mg for men and 310-320 mg for women. Magnesium glycinate and magnesium citrate are preferred formulations due to their high bioavailability.

**B Vitamins:** The RDA varies for each B vitamin. For example, B6 is 1.3-2 mg, B9 is 400 mcg, and B12 is 2.4 mcg per day. A B-complex supplement can be a convenient method to ensure adequate intake of all B vitamins.

**Vitamin D:** The RDA for vitamin D is 600-800 IU per day, but some experts suggest higher dosages, particularly for those with low baseline levels. Blood tests can help determine the appropriate dosage.

**Zinc:** The RDA for zinc is 11 milligrams for men and 8 mg for women. Zinc gluconate and zinc picolinate are preferred formulations for their absorption efficiency.

**Probiotics:** Effective doses of probiotics typically range from 1 billion to 10 billion colony-forming units (CFUs) per day. It is essential to choose a supplement with clinically proven strains.

**L-Theanine:** Typical concentrations range from 100 to 200 mg per day. It can be taken as a supplement or ingested through green tea.

**General Guidelines for Supplement Use**

- Consult a Healthcare Professional: Before commencing any new supplement regimen, particularly if you have underlying health conditions or are taking other medications, consult a healthcare professional.
- Choose High-Quality Products: Ensure that supplements are from reputable manufacturers that provide third-party testing and quality assurance.
- Monitor and Adjust: Regularly monitor your symptoms and overall health while taking supplements. Adjust dosages based on efficacy and any adverse effects encountered, with guidance from a healthcare provider.

# Chapter 5: Alternative Therapies

Alternative therapies offer a variety of approaches to managing anxiety, often complementing traditional methods to provide a holistic strategy for mental well-being. Among these, meditation and mindfulness stand out as highly effective practices. This section examines these practices in detail, emphasizing their benefits and offering guidance on incorporating them into daily life.

## 5.1 Meditation and Mindfulness

Meditation and mindfulness are primordial practices that have garnered substantial recognition in modern psychology and neuroscience for their efficacy in reducing anxiety and promoting overall mental health. Both practices involve cultivating a state of awareness and presence, allowing individuals to observe their thoughts and feelings without judgment.

Practices and Benefits

**Meditation**

Meditation is a practice that entails focusing the mind and eliminating distractions to attain a state of mental clarity and emotional calm. Various modes of meditation can be particularly beneficial for managing anxiety:

- Mindfulness Meditation: This style of meditation entails paying attention to the current moment without judgment. Practitioners focus on their respiration, bodily sensations, or a specific thought or object. The aim is to observe thoughts and sentiments as they arise and let them pass without becoming attached.

- Transcendental Meditation: This technique involves the use of a mantra—a specific word or phrase repeated silently to help focus the mind and attain a profound state of relaxation and heightened awareness.

- Loving-Kindness Meditation: Also known as Metta meditation, this practice involves concentrating on cultivating sentiments of compassion and love towards oneself and others. It can be particularly effective in reducing feelings of apprehension related to social interactions and self-criticism.

**Benefits of Meditation**

The benefits of meditation for anxiety management are well-documented through numerous studies and clinical trials:

- Reduced Stress: Meditation reduces the production of stress hormones such as cortisol, leading to a tranquil and more balanced physiological state.
- Improved Emotional Regulation: Regular meditation practice enhances the ability to manage and regulate emotions, reducing the intensity and frequency of anxiety episodes.
- Enhanced Focus and Concentration: Meditation enhances attention and cognitive function, helping individuals remain present and concentrated, which can mitigate anxious thoughts.
- Better Sleep: By fostering relaxation and reducing tension, meditation can improve sleep quality, which is often disrupted by anxiety.
- Increased Self-Awareness: Meditation fosters a deeper comprehension of oneself, helping individuals recognize and resolve the underlying causes of their anxiety.

**Mindfulness**

Mindfulness involves sustaining a moment-by-moment awareness of thoughts, emotions, bodily sensations, and the surrounding environment. It is about being completely present in the moment and embracing it without judgment.

**Practices of Mindfulness**

- Body Scan: This involves mentally examining the body from head to toe, noting any areas of tension or distress. It serves to bring awareness to somatic sensations and promotes relaxation.
- Breath Awareness: Focusing on the breath is a key mindfulness practice. It entails paying attention to the natural rhythm of breathing and observing the sensation of the breath entering and exiting the body.
- Mindful Walking: This practice entails walking slowly and deliberately, paying attention to the sensations of each stride, the contact of the feet with the ground, and the movements of the body.
- Mindful Eating: Eating mindfully entails devoting complete attention to the experience of eating, and observing the flavors, textures, and sensations of the food. It facilitates a healthy relationship with food and reduces tension around eating.

**Benefits of Mindfulness**

The benefits of mindfulness practices are extensive and supported by an increasing corpus of research:

- Reduced Rumination: Mindfulness helps interrupt the cycle of repetitive, negative thinking that often accompanies anxiety.

- Lower Anxiety Levels: By cultivating a non-judgmental awareness of the present moment, mindfulness reduces the impact of anxiety-provoking thoughts.

- Enhanced Resilience: Mindfulness increases psychological resilience, enabling individuals to manage better with stress and adversity.

- Enhanced physical Health: Regular mindfulness practice has been linked to lower blood pressure, enhanced immune function, and reduced symptoms of chronic pain.

## Guided Sessions

Guided meditation and mindfulness sessions can be particularly beneficial for beginners or those seeking structured practice. These sessions are conducted by experienced practitioners and can be found in various formats, including applications, online videos, and in-person seminars.

**Apps and Online Resources**

Several applications offer guided meditation and mindfulness sessions, making it simple to incorporate these practices into daily life. Here are some prominent options:

- Headspace: This app offers guided meditation sessions for various levels, from beginners to advanced practitioners. It includes programs specifically designed to address anxiety, tension, and sleep issues.

- Calm: Calm provides a variety of guided meditation sessions, mindfulness exercises, and sleep stories. It also features programs focused on anxiety reduction and emotional well-being.

- Insight Timer: This app offers an extensive library of free guided meditations from various instructors and traditions. It includes sessions on mindfulness, tension reduction, and anxiety management.

- 10% Happier: This app concentrates on practical mindfulness and meditation techniques, offering guided sessions that are straightforward and accessible for beginners.

**In-Person Classes and Retreats**

Many communities offer meditation and mindfulness classes through yoga studios, wellness centers, and community organizations for those who prefer in-person guidance. Attending a retreat can also provide an immersive experience, allowing deeper practice and learning.

**Creating a Personal Practice**

Developing a personal meditation and mindfulness practice involves creating a routine that works into your daily existence. Here are some tips for getting started:

- Set Aside Time: Dedicate a specific time each day for meditation or mindfulness practice. Even just 10-15 minutes can make a significant difference.

- Create a Comfortable Space: Choose a tranquil, comfortable space where you can sit or recline down without distractions. Now use cushions or a chair to support your posture.

- Start Small: Begin with short sessions and progressively increase the duration as you become more familiar with the practice.

- Be Patient: Like any talent, meditation, and mindfulness require time to develop. Be compassionate with yourself and recognize that it's normal for the mind to wander.

- Use Resources: Utilize guided sessions and resources to support your practice, particularly in the beginning. These can provide structure and help you remain focused.

## 5.2 Physical Exercise

Physical exercise is a cornerstone of holistic mental health management, offering substantial benefits for reducing anxiety and enhancing overall well-being. This chapter delves into the various forms of exercise and their specific mental health benefits, underscoring the significance of incorporating regular physical activity into a comprehensive anxiety management plan.

## Types of Exercise

Different forms of exercise can uniquely contribute to reducing anxiety and enhancing mental health. Understanding these variations allows individuals to choose the activities that best suit their preferences and lifestyles.

### 1. Aerobic Exercise

Aerobic exercise, also known as cardiovascular exercise, entails sustained, rhythmic activities that increase heart rate and respiration. This form of exercise is highly effective in reducing anxiety and enhancing overall health.

**Examples:** Running, jogging, swimming, cycling, vigorous strolling, and dancing.

**Benefits:** Aerobic exercise increases the release of endorphins—chemicals in the brain that function as natural analgesics and mood elevators. It also enhances cardiovascular health, increases energy levels, and improves sleep, all of which contribute to reducing anxiety.

## 2. Strength Training

Strength training, or resistance training, involves exercises designed to enhance muscle strength and endurance. This form of exercise not only benefits physical health but also has significant mental health advantages.

**Examples:** Weightlifting, bodyweight exercises (such as push-ups and lunges), resistance band exercises, and circuit training.

**Benefits:** Strength training helps reduce symptoms of anxiety by increasing self-esteem and body confidence, relieving tension, and promoting a sense of accomplishment. It also supports improved posture and reduces the risk of chronic discomfort, which can contribute to anxiety.

## 3. Yoga

Yoga incorporates physical postures, breathing exercises, and meditation to create a holistic approach to health and well-being. It is particularly effective for managing anxiety.

**Examples:** Hatha yoga, Vinyasa yoga, Restorative yoga, and Kundalini yoga.

**Benefits:** Yoga promotes relaxation and reduces tension by enhancing the mind-body connection. The practice of mindful movement and deep breathing helps to calm the nervous system, promote flexibility and balance, and cultivate a sense of inner peace.

## 4. Tai Chi and Qigong

Tai Chi and Qigong are ancient Chinese practices that incorporate mild physical movements, meditation, and breathing exercises. They are known for their tranquil and regulating effects on the mind and body.

**Examples:** Traditional Tai Chi forms (such as Yang, Chen, or Wu styles) and various Qigong routines.

**Benefits:** These practices improve mental clarity, reduce tension, and enhance overall well-being. The patient's deliberate movements serve to focus the mind, increase body awareness, and reduce anxiety.

## 5. Pilates

Pilates is a form of exercise that emphasizes abdominal strength, flexibility, and overall body conditioning. It incorporates breathing techniques with precise movements to enhance physical and mental health.

**Examples:** Mat Pilates and Reformer Pilates.

**Benefits:** Pilates helps reduce anxiety by promoting mindfulness, improving posture, and enhancing physical strength and flexibility. The emphasis on controlled respiration and movement fosters a sense of calm and concentration.

## 6. High-Intensity Interval Training (HIIT)

HIIT involves brief bouts of intense exercise alternated with low-intensity recovery periods. It is an efficient method to enhance fitness and mental health.

**Examples:** Sprinting, leaping jacks, burpees, and circuit training with intervals of high effort followed by recovery.

**Benefits:** HIIT can reduce anxiety by releasing endorphins and providing a fast and effective exercise that works into a hectic schedule. The rigorous physical activity also helps to burn off excess energy and reduce tension.

## Mental Health Benefits

Regular physical exercise offers a broad variety of mental health benefits, making it a powerful tool for managing anxiety. Here are some important benefits:

### 1. Reduction in Anxiety Symptoms

Exercise is a natural and effective anti-anxiety treatment. It decreases symptoms by controlling levels of the body's stress chemicals, such as adrenaline and cortisol. Regular physical activity also enhances the production of endorphins, which are chemicals in the brain that function as natural painkillers and mood elevators.

### 2. Improved Mood and Emotional Well-being

Physical activity enhances the release of neurotransmitters like serotonin and dopamine, which play crucial roles in modulating mood and emotion. This leads to enhanced mood, reduced symptoms of depression, and a general sense of well-being.

### 3. Enhanced Cognitive Function

Exercise improves cognitive function by increasing blood flow to the brain, which enhances memory, concentration, and problem-solving abilities. It also promotes the growth of new brain cells and enhances the connectivity between various brain regions.

### 4. Better Sleep Quality

Regular physical activity can help modulate sleep patterns, leading to improved sleep quality. Improved sleep reduces fatigue, enhances mood, and decreases anxiety levels. Exercise, particularly when performed earlier in the day, can help establish a healthy sleep routine.

### 5. Increased Self-Esteem and Confidence

Engaging in regular exercise enhances physical endurance and body image, leading to increased self-esteem and confidence. This positive self-perception can reduce social anxiety and enhance overall mental health.

### 6. Stress Reduction

Exercise is a potent tension reliever. It serves to relax tense muscles, enhance circulation, and reduce the physical symptoms of stress. The act of concentrating on physical movement also provides a mental break from concerns and stressors.

**7. Social Interaction and Support**

Participating in group exercises or team sports offers opportunities for social interaction and support. Building social connections and a sense of community can ameliorate feelings of loneliness and isolation, which are often associated with anxiety.

**8. Mindfulness and Presence**

Certain forms of exercise, such as yoga, Tai Chi, and Pilates, incorporate elements of mindfulness and meditation. These practices help individuals focus on the present moment, reducing rumination and apprehensive thoughts.

**Implementing an Exercise Routine**

To maximize the mental health benefits of exercise, it is essential to establish a consistent and pleasurable routine. Here are some tips for getting started:

- Set Realistic objectives: Start with modest, achievable objectives and progressively increase the intensity and duration of your workouts. Setting realistic objectives helps maintain motivation and prevents fatigue.

- Find Activities You Enjoy: Now choose exercises that you enjoy and look forward to. Whether it's dancing, hiking, swimming, or performing a sport, finding delight in the activity increases the likelihood of maintaining a routine.

- Schedule Regular Exercise: Dedicate specific times each week for exercise, and approach these appointments with the same importance as other commitments. Consistency is essential to obtaining the long-term benefits.

- Mix It Up: Incorporate a variety of exercises to keep your routine intriguing and well-rounded. Mixing aerobic, strength, flexibility, and mindfulness exercises can provide comprehensive benefits.

- Listen to Your Body: Pay attention to your body's signals and modify your routine as required. It's essential to balance effort with rest and recovery to prevent injury and maintain overall health.

- Seek Support: Join exercise classes, or sports teams, or locate a workout partner to provide social support and accountability. Sharing the experience can enhance motivation and enjoyment.

## 5.3 Yoga and Tai Chi

Yoga and Tai Chi are ancient practices that integrate physical movement, respiration control, and meditation to promote holistic well-being. Both practices have been shown to substantially reduce anxiety and enhance overall mental health. This section examines the techniques and routines of Yoga and Tai Chi and offers guidance on integrating these practices into daily life.

## Techniques and Routines

**Yoga**

Yoga is a comprehensive practice that incorporates physical postures (asanas), respiration control (pranayama), and meditation (dhyana) to enhance physical, mental, and emotional health. There are various varieties of yoga, each with its unique focus and benefits.

**1. Hatha Yoga**

Hatha Yoga is a gentle practice that emphasizes fundamental postures and respiration control. It is suitable for beginners and those seeking to reduce anxiety through relaxation and mindfulness.

**Techniques:**

- Mountain Pose (Tadasana): A grounding posture that promotes stability and serenity.
- Child's Pose (Balasana): A restorative pose that relieves stress and tension.
- Corpse Pose (Savasana): A relaxation pose that facilitates deep respiration and mental clarity.

**Routine:** A typical Hatha Yoga routine involves a series of sluggish, deliberate movements combined with profound breathing. Start with a warm-up, progress through a sequence of standing and seated poses, and conclude with a relaxation pose.

## 2. Vinyasa Yoga

Vinyasa Yoga is a dynamic practice that connects respiration with movement, generating a flowing sequence of postures. It is superb for building strength, flexibility, and mental focus.

**Techniques:**

- Sun Salutations (Surya Namaskar): A series of poses performed in a continuous sequence to soften up the body.
- Warrior Poses (Virabhadrasana I, II, III): Strength-building poses that enhance focus and resilience.
- Downward-Facing Dog (Adho Mukha Svanasana): A foundational pose that stretches and strengthens the body.

**Routine:** A Vinyasa Yoga routine typically begins with Sun Salutations to warm up, followed by a series of standing and balancing poses, and concludes with seated stretches and a relaxation pose.

## 3. Restorative Yoga

Restorative Yoga focuses on profound relaxation and tension relief. Poses are held for extended periods, often with the support of objects, to encourage complete physical and mental release.

### Techniques:

- Supported Bridge Pose (Setu Bandhasana): A mild backbend that opens the ribcage and reduces tension.
- Legs-Up-the-Wall Pose (Viparita Karani): A tranquil inversion that relaxes the nervous system.
- Reclining Bound Angle Pose (Supta Baddha Konasana): A restorative hip opener that promotes relaxation.

**Routine:** A Restorative Yoga routine involves a few poses sustained for several minutes each, concentrating on deep breathing and mental relaxation. Props such as bolsters, comforters, and blocks are used for support.

## Tai Chi

Tai Chi is a Chinese martial art known for its leisurely, fluid movements and meditative focus. It is often characterized as "meditation in motion" and is highly effective in reducing anxiety and promoting balance and harmony.

**1. Yang Style Tai Chi**

Yang Yang-style tai Chi is the most widely practiced form, characterized by its leisurely, graceful movements and large, expansive gestures.

**Techniques:**

- Commencement (Qi Shi): The opening movement that establishes the tone for the practice.
- Parting the Horse's Mane (Ye Ma Fen Zong): A graceful movement that promotes balance and coordination.
- Grasp the Bird's Tail (Lan Que Wei): A sequence of movements that enhance strength and flexibility.

**Routine:** A Yang Style Tai Chi routine typically begins with a warm-up, followed by a sequence of flowing movements performed methodically and mindfully. The practice concludes with a cool-down to incorporate the benefits.

**2. Chen Style Tai Chi**

Chen Chen-style tai Chi is characterized by its variegated tempo and explosive movements, making it more physically demanding. It incorporates slow, flowing movements with rapid, forceful ones.

**Techniques:**

- Silk Reeling (Chan Si Gong): Circular movements that develop strength and flexibility.
- Cannon Fist (Pao Chui): Fast, explosive movements that build power and resilience.
- Single Whip (Dan Bian): A foundational movement that enhances coordination and balance.

**Routine:** A Chen Chen-style tai Chi routine involves a combination of calm, meditative movements and rapid, powerful actions. The practice emphasizes continuous, circular motion and coordination between the upper and lower body.

## Integration into Daily Life

Incorporating Yoga and Tai Chi into daily life can provide enduring benefits for mental health and overall well-being. Here are some strategies for integrating these practices seamlessly into your routine:

### 1. Establish a Regular Practice

Consistency is essential to obtaining the benefits of Yoga and Tai Chi. Establish a consistent practice routine that matches your lifestyle.

- Set a Time: Choose a specific time each day for your practice. Morning sessions can set a positive tone for the day, while evening sessions can help decompress and calm before bed.
- Create a Space: Designate a tranquil, comfortable space in your residence for your practice. Ensure it is free from distractions and conducive to relaxation and focus.

## 2. Start Small and Build Gradually

If you are new to Yoga or Tai Chi, commence with short sessions and progressively increase the duration and complexity of your practice.

- Begin with Basics: Start with fundamental poses and movements, focusing on appropriate form and breath control. As you become more familiar, introduce more advanced techniques.
- Incremental Progress: Gradually extend your practice time and incorporate more challenging routines as your skills and confidence grow.

## 3. Use Guided Resources

Utilize guided resources such as online classes, applications, and videos to support your practice. These resources can provide structure, instruction, and motivation.

- Online Classes: Platforms like YouTube, Glo, and Gaia offer a wide range of Yoga and Tai Chi classes for all levels.
- Apps: Apps like Down Dog (Yoga) and Tai Chi Trainer provide guided sessions and customizable routines.
- Instructional Videos: Follow along with instructional videos to ensure proper technique and remain motivated.

**4. Integrate Mindfulness**

Both Yoga and Tai Chi emphasize mindfulness, which can enhance the mental health benefits of the practices.

Focus on respiration: Pay attention to your respiration throughout your practice. Deep, deliberate breathing can enhance relaxation and focus.

Be Present: Cultivate awareness of the present moment, observing your movements, sensations, and thoughts without judgment.

# Chapter 6: Effects of Drugs on Anxiety

Pharmacological interventions play a significant role in the management of anxiety disorders, particularly when symptoms are severe or resistant to other forms of treatment. This section provides a detailed overview of prescription medications commonly used to treat anxiety, investigating their types, mechanisms of action, benefits, and potential adverse effects.

## 6.1 Prescription Medications

Prescription medications for anxiety are diverse, comprising several classes that target various neurotransmitter systems in the brain. These medications can provide significant respite from anxiety symptoms, but they must be carefully managed due to potential adverse effects and the risk of dependency.

### Types of Medications

**Selective Serotonin Reuptake Inhibitors (SSRIs)**

SSRIs are a genus of antidepressants that are often first-line therapies for anxiety disorders. They work by enhancing the levels of serotonin, a neurotransmitter that regulates mood, in the brain.

- Common SSRIs: Fluoxetine (Prozac), Sertraline (Zoloft), Escitalopram (Lexapro), Paroxetine (Paxil), and Citalopram (Celexa).
- Mechanism of Action: SSRIs inhibit the reuptake of serotonin into presynaptic neurons, increasing its availability in the synaptic cleft and enhancing serotonergic neurotransmission.

**Serotonin-Norepinephrine Reuptake Inhibitors (SNRIs)**

SNRIs are another class of antidepressants that are effective in treating anxiety disorders. They boost the levels of both serotonin and norepinephrine in the brain.

- Common SNRIs: Venlafaxine (Effexor), Duloxetine (Cymbalta), and Desvenlafaxine (Pristiq).
- Mechanism of Action: SNRIs inhibit the reuptake of serotonin and norepinephrine, enhancing the activity of these neurotransmitters and alleviating mood and anxiety symptoms.

**Benzodiazepines**

Benzodiazepines are fast-acting anxiolytics commonly used for short-term relief of severe anxiety symptoms. They are notably efficacious in acute anxiety episodes and panic attacks.

- Common Benzodiazepines: Diazepam (Valium), Lorazepam (Ativan), Clonazepam (Klonopin), and Alprazolam (Xanax).
- Mechanism of Action: Benzodiazepines enhance the effect of the neurotransmitter gamma-aminobutyric acid (GABA) at the GABA-A receptor, leading to increased inhibitory effects and generating a soothing effect on the brain.

### Beta-Blockers

Beta-blockers are predominantly used to manage cardiovascular conditions but can also be effective in managing the physical symptoms of anxiety, such as rapid pulse and trembling.

- Common Beta-Blockers: Propranolol (Inderal) and Atenolol (Tenormin).
- Mechanism of Action: Beta-blockers block the effects of adrenaline on beta receptors, reducing physical symptoms of anxiety by slowing the pulse rate and decreasing blood pressure.

### Tricyclic Antidepressants (TCAs)

TCAs are an ancient class of antidepressants that are sometimes used to treat anxiety disorders, particularly when SSRIs and SNRIs are ineffective.

- Common TCAs: Amitriptyline (Elavil), Imipramine (Tofranil), and Clomipramine (Anafranil).
- Mechanism of Action: TCAs inhibit the reuptake of serotonin and norepinephrine, similar to SNRIs, but they also affect other neurotransmitters, which can contribute to a broader range of adverse effects.

**Monoamine Oxidase Inhibitors (MAOIs)**

MAOIs are another ancient class of antidepressants used to treat anxiety disorders, particularly when other medications are not efficacious. They necessitate dietary restrictions to avoid potentially hazardous interactions.

- Common MAOIs: Phenelzine (Nardil), Tranylcypromine (Parnate), and Isocarboxazid (Marplan).
- Mechanism of Action: MAOIs inhibit the enzyme monoamine oxidase, which breaks down neurotransmitters such as serotonin, norepinephrine, and dopamine, thereby increasing their levels in the brain.

**Atypical Antipsychotics**

Atypical antipsychotics are sometimes used as adjunctive therapies for anxiety disorders, particularly when other medications are insufficient.

- Common Atypical Antipsychotics: Quetiapine (Seroquel), Aripiprazole (Abilify), and Olanzapine (Zyprexa).
- Mechanism of Action: These medications act on numerous neurotransmitter receptors, including dopamine and serotonin receptors, to stabilize mood and reduce anxiety symptoms.

## Benefits and Side Effects

While prescription medications can be highly effective in managing anxiety, they come with potential benefits and adverse effects that must be carefully considered.

### 1. Selective Serotonin Reuptake Inhibitors (SSRIs)

**Benefits:** SSRIs are commonly well-tolerated and effective in reducing symptoms of anxiety. They have a lower risk of dependency compared to benzodiazepines.

**Side Effects:** Common side effects include vertigo, dizziness, insomnia, sexual dysfunction, and weight gain. Some individuals may experience increased apprehension during the initial weeks of treatment.

## 2. Serotonin-Norepinephrine Reuptake Inhibitors (SNRIs)

**Benefits:** SNRIs can be particularly effective for individuals who do not respond to SSRIs. They also help mitigate physical discomfort, which can be associated with anxiety.

**Side Effects:** Common side effects include vertigo, parched mouth, disorientation, sweating, and sexual dysfunction. There may be an initial increase in anxiety symptoms.

## 3. Benzodiazepines

**Benefits:** Benzodiazepines provide rapid relief of anxiety symptoms and are effective in acute situations such as panic attacks.

**Side Effects:** Common side effects include lethargy, vertigo, confusion, and impaired coordination. Long-term usage can develop tolerance, reliance, and withdrawal symptoms upon termination.

## 4. Beta-Blockers

**Benefits:** Beta-blockers are effective in reducing physical symptoms of anxiety, such as tremors and palpitations, and can be used as required for situational anxiety.

**Side Effects:** Common side effects include fatigue, frigid extremities, disorientation, and sleep disturbances. They are not typically used for long-term anxiety management due to their limited effect on psychological symptoms.

## 5. Tricyclic Antidepressants (TCAs)

**Benefits:** TCAs can be effective for anxiety, particularly when other medications fail. They also assist with chronic pain conditions that can co-occur with anxiety.

**Side Effects:** Common side effects include parched mouth, constipation, urinary retention, blurred vision, weight gain, and lethargy. TCAs have a higher risk of cardiovascular effects and are generally considered less safe than SSRIs and SNRIs.

## 6. Monoamine Oxidase Inhibitors (MAOIs)

**Benefits:** MAOIs can be effective for treatment-resistant anxiety disorders. They provide significant symptom relief for some individuals.

**Side Effects:** Common side effects include vertigo, parched mouth, insomnia, weight gain, and sexual dysfunction. MAOIs require stringent dietary restrictions to avoid hypertensive crises induced by foods containing tyramine.

## 7. Atypical Antipsychotics

**Benefits:** Atypical antipsychotics can be effective as adjunctive therapies for anxiety, particularly in cases with co-occurring mood disorders or when other medications are inadequate.

**Side Effects:** Common side effects include weight gain, metabolic alterations, lethargy, and increased risk of diabetes. Long-term use can lead to movement disorders such as tardive dyskinesia.

**Considerations for Use**

When contemplating pharmacological treatment for anxiety, it is crucial to weigh the benefits and risks thoroughly. Here are some important considerations:

- Individual Response: Individuals may respond differently to medications, and finding the correct medication often requires trial and error under medical supervision.
- Side Effect Management: Managing side effects is crucial for maintaining treatment adherence. Regular monitoring and communication with a healthcare provider can help address any adverse effects.
- Duration of Treatment: Some medications, particularly benzodiazepines, are intended for short-term use due to the danger of dependency. Others, like SSRIs and SNRIs, may be used long-term.
- Combination Therapy: In some cases, a combination of medications may be necessary for optimal symptom control. A healthcare professional should always manage this.
- Lifestyle Integration: Medications should be part of a comprehensive treatment plan that includes lifestyle adjustments, therapy, and alternative therapies to address the underlying causes of anxiety.

## 6.2 Over-the-Counter Alternatives

In addition to prescription medications, numerous over-the-counter (OTC) alternatives can assist in the management of mild to moderate anxiety symptoms. These alternatives are more readily available and typically exhibit fewer adverse effects than prescription medications. Nevertheless, it is imperative to comprehend their usage, effectiveness, risks, and precautions to guarantee optimal and safe results.

### Effectiveness and Usage

Over-the-counter options for anxiety management typically include dietary supplements and herbal remedies. Although these alternatives may be advantageous, their effectiveness may fluctuate contingent on the product's quality and the individual's response.

**1. Dietary Supplements**

**L-Theanine**

L-Theanine is an amino acid present in green tea, known for its soothing effects without inducing drowsiness.

**Usage:** L-Theanine is available in capsule or tablet form and is typically consumed in concentrations of 100-200 mg, up to twice daily.

**Effectiveness:** Research suggests that L-Theanine can promote relaxation and reduce tension by increasing levels of serotonin and dopamine in the brain. It also enhances alpha brain wave activity, associated with a state of relaxed alertness.

## Magnesium

Magnesium is a vital mineral involved in numerous biochemical processes, including nerve function and muscle relaxation.

**Usage:** Magnesium supplements are available in various forms, such as magnesium citrate, magnesium glycinate, and magnesium oxide. The typical dosage ranges from 200-400 mg per day, depending on individual requirements and tolerability.

**Effectiveness:** Magnesium has been shown to ameliorate anxiety symptoms by modulating the activity of the hypothalamic-pituitary-adrenal (HPA) axis and enhancing GABAergic function.

## Vitamin B Complex

vitamins B, particularly B6, B9 (folate), and B12, are essential for neurotransmitter synthesis and overall brain health.

**Usage:** Vitamin B complex supplements, which include all essential B vitamins, are commonly taken once daily according to the recommended dietary allowance (RDA) for each vitamin.

**Effectiveness:** Adequate levels of B vitamins support the production of serotonin and dopamine, helping to modulate mood and reduce anxiety.

## 2. Herbal Remedies

### Valerian Root

Valerian root is a botanical traditionally used to alleviate insomnia and anxiety. It is known for its sedative properties.

**Usage:** Valerian root is available in capsule, tablet, and tincture forms. The typical dosage ranges from 400-900 mg of valerian extract, administered 30 minutes to two hours before slumber.

**Effectiveness:** Studies indicate that valerian root can help improve sleep quality and reduce anxiety by increasing GABA levels in the brain.

### Passionflower

Passionflower is a herb used for its soothing effects and ability to assuage anxiety.

**Usage:** Passionflower can be consumed as a tea, tincture, or capsule. The typical dosage is 200-400 mg of extract or 1-2 grams of desiccated herb up to three times daily.

**Effectiveness:** Passionflower has been shown to enhance GABAergic activity, thereby promoting relaxation and reducing anxiety symptoms.

**Chamomile**

Chamomile is a well-known herb used for its moderate sedative and anxiolytic properties.

**Usage:** Chamomile is commonly ingested as a tea, with 1-2 teaspoons of dried flowers steeped in boiling water for 5-10 minutes. Chamomile extract capsules are also available, typically consumed in concentrations of 220-1100 mg daily.

**Effectiveness:** Chamomile contains apigenin, a compound that attaches to benzodiazepine receptors in the brain, producing a tranquil effect.

## Risks and Precautions

While over-the-counter options can offer respite from anxiety symptoms, it is essential to be aware of potential risks and precautions associated with their use.

## 1. Dietary Supplements

### L-Theanine

**Risks:** L-theanine is generally well-tolerated, but excessive quantities may induce headaches, dizziness, or gastrointestinal distress.

**Precautions:** Consult with a healthcare provider before commencing L-Theanine, particularly if you are pregnant, breastfeeding, or taking other medications.

### Magnesium

**Risks:** High quantities of magnesium can cause diarrhea, vertigo, and abdominal discomfort. Individuals with kidney disease should avoid magnesium supplements due to the risk of hypermagnesemia.

**Precautions:** Start with a lesser dose to assess tolerance and progressively increase as required. Consult with a healthcare practitioner before usage, particularly if you have any underlying health concerns.

### Vitamin B Complex

**Risks:** High concentrations of certain vitamins B, particularly B6, can cause nerve injury or other adverse effects. Most B vitamins are water-soluble, and surplus quantities are excreted in urine, but excessive intake should still be avoided.

**Precautions:** Follow the recommended dosage and consult with a healthcare provider before commencing a vitamin B complex supplement, particularly if you have any underlying health conditions.

## 2. Herbal Remedies

### Valerian Root

**Risks:** Valerian root may cause drowsiness, vertigo, or gastrointestinal distress. Long-term use can lead to dependency or withdrawal symptoms.

**Precautions:** Avoid using valerian root with alcohol or other sedatives. Consult with a healthcare provider before use, particularly if you are pregnant, lactating, or taking other medications.

### Passionflower

**Risks:** Passionflower is generally safe, but excessive quantities can cause vertigo, confusion, or sedation. Allergic reactions are also conceivable.

**Precautions:** Do not combine passionflower with other sedative medications or alcohol. Consult with a healthcare provider before use, particularly if you are pregnant, lactating, or taking other medications.

**Chamomile**

**Risks:** Chamomile is generally safe but can induce allergic reactions in individuals sensitive to ragweed or other related plants. High concentrations may cause nausea or vomiting.

**Precautions:** Avoid chamomile if you have severe allergies to pollen. Consult with a healthcare provider before use, particularly if you are pregnant, lactating, or taking other medications.

**General Considerations for Over-the-Counter Options**

- Quality and Purity: Choose high-quality supplements and herbal remedies from reputable manufacturers to ensure purity and potency. Look for items that have been independently tested and verified.

- Consultation with Healthcare Providers: Always consult with a healthcare provider before commencing any new supplement or herbal remedy, particularly if you have existing health conditions or are taking other medications. This serves to prevent potential interactions and ensures safe usage.

- Dosage and Duration: Follow the recommended dosages and be mindful of the duration of use. Some supplements and herbal remedies may be secure for short-term use but could pose risks if taken long-term.

## 6.3 Substance Use and Anxiety

The relationship between substance use and anxiety is complex and multifaceted. While individuals may use substances such as alcohol and recreational drugs to self-medicate and alleviate anxiety symptoms temporarily, these substances often exacerbate anxiety over time. This section analyzes the impact of alcohol and recreational substances on anxiety and provides strategies for reduction and cessation to promote long-term mental health.

### Impact of Alcohol and Recreational Drugs

**Alcohol**

Alcohol is a central nervous system depressant that can generate transient sensations of relaxation and euphoria. However, its effects on anxiety are paradoxical and often detrimental in the long term.

- Initial Effects: Alcohol can temporarily reduce anxiety by increasing the activity of gamma-aminobutyric acid (GABA), an inhibitory neurotransmitter that promotes relaxation and decreases neural excitability. This can contribute to a temporary sensation of calm and reduced anxiety.

- **Long-term Effects:** Chronic alcohol use disrupts the balance of neurotransmitters in the brain, resulting in increased anxiety. Tolerance and dependence can develop, requiring higher quantities of alcohol to achieve the same effects, which can exacerbate anxiety symptoms and contribute to a cycle of dependence.
- **Withdrawal:** Alcohol withdrawal can produce severe anxiety, agitation, and panic attacks. In severe cases, withdrawal can lead to delirium tremens, a life-threatening condition characterized by disorientation, convulsions, and hallucinations.

**Recreational Drugs**

Recreational drugs, including stimulants, hallucinogens, and opioids, can have substantial and diverse impacts on anxiety.

- **Stimulants:** Drugs such as cocaine, amphetamines, and methamphetamines increase levels of dopamine and norepinephrine in the brain, leading to heightened arousal and euphoria. However, these medications can also cause increased anxiety, paranoia, and panic attacks, particularly as their effects fade off.
- **Hallucinogens:** Substances like LSD, psilocybin (magic mushrooms), and MDMA (ecstasy) alter perception and mood by acting on serotonin receptors. While some users may experience temporary relief from anxiety, these substances can also induce anxiety, confusion, and

hallucinations, particularly at high dosages or during "bad trips."

- Opioids: Drugs such as heroin, morphine, and prescription analgesics (e.g., oxycodone) elicit potent sensations of euphoria and relaxation by binding to opioid receptors in the brain. Chronic use can lead to tolerance, dependency, and increased anxiety, particularly during withdrawal, which can cause severe anxiety, agitation, and physical symptoms.

## Strategies for Reduction and Cessation

Reducing or ceasing the use of alcohol and recreational substances is crucial for managing anxiety and enhancing overall mental health. The following strategies can support individuals in attaining and maintaining sobriety:

**1. Assessment and Planning**

**Self-Assessment:** Begin with an honest assessment of substance use and its impact on anxiety and overall well-being. Identify patterns of use, triggers, and consequences.

**Professional Evaluation:** Consult a healthcare professional or addiction specialist for a comprehensive evaluation and to develop a personalized reduction or cessation plan.

**2. Gradual Reduction

**Tapering:** Gradually reducing the quantity of the substance used can help mitigate withdrawal symptoms and make the process more manageable. This approach is particularly essential for substances with severe withdrawal syndromes, such as alcohol and narcotics.

**Monitoring Progress**: Monitor usage, symptoms, and progress in a journal. Regularly review and alter the reduction plan as required, with the guidance of a healthcare provider.

### 3. Behavioral Therapies

**Cognitive Behavioral Therapy (CBT):** CBT helps individuals identify and challenge negative thought patterns and behaviors related to substance use and anxiety. It provides coping strategies and instruments to manage triggers and cravings.

**Motivational Interviewing (MI):** MI is a client-centered approach that enhances motivation and commitment to change. It helps individuals examine and resolve ambivalence about reducing or ceasing substance use.

### 4. Support Systems

**Support Groups:** Participation in support groups such as Alcoholics Anonymous (AA), Narcotics Anonymous (NA), or SMART Recovery provides a sense of community and shared experience. These communities offer peer support, accountability, and encouragement.

**Family and colleagues:** Engage family and colleagues in the recovery process. Their support and understanding can provide additional motivation and stability.

## 5. Medication-Assisted Treatment (MAT)

**Pharmacotherapy:** Medications can help manage withdrawal symptoms, reduce cravings, and support long-term recovery. Examples include naltrexone, acamprosate, and disulfiram for alcohol dependence and methadone, buprenorphine, and naltrexone for opioid dependence.

**Monitoring and Support:** Regular monitoring and support from healthcare providers can ensure the safe and effective use of medications as part of a comprehensive treatment plan.

## 6. Lifestyle Changes

**Healthy Diet and Exercise:** A balanced diet and regular physical activity can improve mood, reduce anxiety, and enhance overall well-being. Exercise, in particular, has been shown to reduce tension and enhance mental health.

**Mindfulness and Relaxation Techniques:** Practices such as mindfulness meditation, yoga, and deep breathing exercises can help manage tension and anxiety, reducing the reliance on substances for relief.

**Structured Routine:** Establishing a planned daily routine can give stability and lessen the chance of recurrence. Include time for self-care, interests, and activities that promote relaxation and enjoyment.

## 7. Professional Support

**Therapists and Counselors:** Regular sessions with therapists or counselors who specialize in addiction and anxiety can provide continuous support and guidance throughout the recovery process.

**Healthcare Providers:** Regular check-ins with healthcare providers can monitor physical health, manage any medical conditions, and modify treatment plans as required.

## 8. Relapse Prevention

**Identify Triggers:** Recognize and avoid situations, people, and environments that trigger substance use. Develop strategies to contend with unavoidable triggers.

**Emergency Plan:** Have a plan in place for managing cravings and potential relapses. This may include contacting a support person, attending a meeting, or using coping techniques learned in therapy.

**Ongoing Support:** Continue to engage in support groups, therapy, and healthy lifestyle practices even after attaining sobriety to maintain long-term recovery and manage anxiety.

# Chapter 7: Community and Support

A robust community and support network can play a pivotal role in managing anxiety. Online platforms like Reddit offer a space where individuals can share their experiences, seek advice, and find solace in knowing they are not alone. This section examines anxiety hacks from Reddit, highlighting popular tactics, advice, and real-life success stories that have resonated with many.

## 7.1 Anxiety Hacks from Reddit

Reddit, a prominent online community, has numerous subreddits dedicated to mental health, where users discuss their strategies for managing anxiety. These platforms provide a plethora of collective knowledge and support, offering practical advice and emotional encouragement. Here, we delve into some of the most popular advice and real-life success stories shared by Reddit users.

### Popular Tips and Advice

## 1. Grounding Techniques

Grounding techniques are frequently recommended by Reddit users for their efficacy in managing acute anxiety. These techniques help individuals focus on the present moment, reducing the intensity of apprehensive thoughts and emotions.

- The 5-4-3-2-1 Technique: This method involves using the five senses to ground oneself. Users are encouraged to identify five things they can see, four things they can touch, three things they can hear, two things they can smell, and one thing they can taste. This exercise can rapidly divert attention from anxiety to the immediate environment, promoting serenity.
- Object Focus: Some users propose carrying a small, textured object like a polished stone or a fidget device. When anxiety strikes, concentrating on the object's texture and shape can provide a sensory distraction and reduce anxiety.

## 2. Breathing Exercises

Controlled breathing is a potent instrument for managing anxiety, and many Reddit users emphasize its importance.

- Box Breathing: This technique involves inhaling for four seconds, holding the breath for four seconds, exhaling for four seconds, and holding the breath out for four seconds.

Repeating this cycle helps regulate respiration and calm the nervous system.

- Deep Diaphragmatic Breathing: Users recommend placing one hand on the chest and the other on the abdomen, breathing deeply so that the abdomen raises and descends. This form of respiration encourages full oxygen exchange and can reduce the physical symptoms of anxiety.

## 3. Cognitive Behavioral Techniques

Cognitive Behavioral Therapy (CBT) techniques are also commonly shared on Reddit as effective methods to manage anxiety.

- Thought Challenging: Users suggest identifying and challenging negative thoughts by asking queries such as, "What evidence do I have for this thought?" and "What would I tell a friend in this situation?" This technique helps reframe irrational thoughts into more balanced perspectives.
- Journaling: Keeping a journal to document thoughts and emotions can help individuals identify patterns and triggers. Writing down concerns and then rational responses to those worries can also provide relief.

## 4. Mindfulness and Meditation

Mindfulness and meditation practices are frequently recommended for their long-term benefits in reducing anxiety.

- Guided Meditations: Many users find guided meditation apps like Headspace, Calm, and Insight Timer beneficial. These applications offer structured sessions that teach mindfulness and meditation techniques.
- Mindful Activities: Incorporating mindfulness into daily activities, such as mindful dining or mindful walking, can help individuals remain present and reduce anxiety throughout the day.

**5. Physical Activity**

Regular physical activity is another prevalent recommendation on Reddit for managing anxiety.

- Exercise Routines: Users share their experiences with various forms of exercise, such as running, yoga, and calisthenics. Physical activity helps release endorphins, which can enhance mood and reduce tension.
- Daily Walks: Many users find that even a brief daily walk can significantly reduce anxiety levels, providing both physical and mental benefits.

## Real-life Success Stories

## 1. Overcoming Social Anxiety

Sampson shared his journey of overcoming social anxiety through a combination of exposure therapy and community support. Initially, even minor social interactions created intense anxiety. By progressively exposing themselves to more challenging social situations and receiving encouragement from the Reddit community, they were able to develop confidence and reduce their anxiety. Today, they participate in social events and engage in conversations with ease, crediting their progress to the supportive feedback and practical advice they received online.

## 2. Managing Panic Attacks

Naomi recounted her struggle with frequent panic attacks and how she found solace in the shared experiences on Reddit. She discovered grounding techniques, such as the 5-4-3-2-1 method, which helped them regain control during an attack. Additionally, she incorporated breathing exercises into her daily regimen, which reduced the frequency and severity of his panic attacks. The emotional support and understanding she discovered on Reddit were instrumental in her quest to manage and eventually overcome her panic attacks.

## 3. Finding Stability Through Routine

Fredo revealed how establishing a daily routine transformed his life. Struggling with generalized anxiety disorder, he found it challenging to manage day-to-day tasks. By implementing suggestions from Reddit, such as setting a consistent sleep schedule, planning meals, and incorporating regular exercise, he created a structured routine that provided stability and reduced his anxiety. The support and encouragement from the Reddit community helped him remain committed to these adjustments, leading to significant improvements in his mental health.

## 4. Healing Through Creativity

Ruth found that engaging in creative activities was a potent channel for her anxiety. She began with adult coloring books and progressively moved on to painting and writing. Sharing his artwork and tales on Reddit not only provided an emotional release but also connected her with others who appreciated and supported their creative journey. This engagement helped them analyze their emotions and manage their anxiety more effectively.

## 5. Building a Supportive Network

John emphasized the significance of building a supportive network, both online and offline. He shared his experience of joining local support groups for persons with anxiety and supplementing this with participation in Reddit discussions. This dual approach provided a comprehensive support system, offering practical advice and emotional reassurance. Over time, they developed stronger coping mechanisms and significantly reduced their anxiety symptoms.

## 7.2 Building a Support System

A comprehensive support system is crucial for effectively managing anxiety and nurturing long-term mental well-being. Engaging with support groups and seeking professional assistance are two important components of building such a system. This chapter delves into how to locate and utilize support groups and when and how to seek professional assistance.

### Finding and Utilizing Support Groups

Support groups provide a platform for individuals to share their experiences, receive encouragement, and obtain insights from others facing similar challenges. These organizations can be found both online and offline, offering flexible options to suit different needs and preferences.

### 1. Identifying the Right Support Group

Finding the correct support group is essential for deriving the maximum benefit. Consider the following factors when selecting a group:

- Focus and Relevance: Choose a group specifically tailored to anxiety or related mental health issues. Groups concentrating on generalized anxiety disorder (GAD), social anxiety, panic disorder, or other specific concerns can provide more targeted support.

- Format: Determine whether you prefer in-person meetings, online forums, or virtual group sessions. Each format has its advantages—online groups offer convenience and anonymity, while in-person meetings can provide a more personal connection.

- Size and Structure: Consider the magnitude of the group and its meeting structure. Smaller groups may offer more intimate and personalized support, while larger groups can provide diverse perspectives and resources.

### 2. Utilizing Support Groups Effectively

Once you have identified a suitable support group, actively engaging with the group is crucial to realizing its benefits:

- Regular Participation: Attend meetings or participate in discussions regularly to develop a sense of community and continuity. Consistent engagement helps foster trust and deeper connections with group members.

- Active Listening and Sharing: Practice active listening to understand and empathize with others' experiences. Sharing your own experiences, challenges, and successes can provide relief and promote mutual support.

- Leveraging Resources: Many support groups offer additional resources, such as educational materials, seminars, and guest speakers. Take advantage of these opportunities to enhance your understanding and management of anxiety.

**Examples of Support Groups**

- Local Support Groups: Check community centers, hospitals, and mental health organizations for local support groups. The Anxiety and Depression Association of America (ADAA) and the National Alliance on Mental Illness (NAMI) offer directories for locating local groups.
- Online Communities: Websites like Reddit, Mental Health America, and HealthUnlocked host active forums and support groups where individuals can share their experiences and receive advice.
- Virtual Group Therapy: Many mental health professionals offer virtual group therapy sessions, providing structured support from a licensed therapist in a group setting.

## Professional Help: When and How to Seek It

While support groups can provide valuable interpersonal support, professional assistance is essential for a comprehensive approach to managing anxiety. Recognizing when and how to obtain professional assistance can significantly improve outcomes.

**1. Recognizing the Need for Professional Help**

Consider seeking professional aid if you experience any of the following:

- Persistent Symptoms: If anxiety symptoms persist for an extended period (e.g., several months) and interfere with daily functioning, professional intervention may be necessary.
- Severe Anxiety: Intense anxiety that leads to panic attacks, phobias, or severe physical symptoms should be addressed by a mental health professional.
- Impact on Quality of Life: When anxiety negatively affects relationships, work performance, or overall quality of life, it is crucial to seek professional support.
- Co-occurring Disorders: If anxiety coexists with other mental health conditions, such as depression or substance use disorder, a comprehensive treatment plan from a professional is essential.

## 2. Types of Professional Help

Different kinds of professionals can provide numerous forms of treatment and support for anxiety:

- Psychologists: Specialize in psychotherapy and behavioral interventions. They can help you develop coping strategies, change negative thought patterns, and address underlying psychological issues.

- Psychiatrists: Medical physicians who can diagnose and treat mental health conditions, often using medication management in conjunction with psychotherapy.
- Licensed Professional Counselors (LPCs): Provide therapy and counseling to help manage anxiety through various therapeutic modalities.
- Social Workers: Offer counseling and support services, often with a concentration on connecting clients to community resources and support systems.

### 3. How to Seek Professional Help

Taking the first step towards seeking professional assistance can be daunting. Here are some guidelines to facilitate the process:

- Research and Referrals: Start by researching professionals in your area. Ask for referrals from primary care physicians, trusted colleagues or family members, or support group leaders. Online directories from organizations like the American Psychological Association (APA) and the National Institute of Mental Health (NIMH) can also be helpful.
- Initial Consultation: Schedule an initial consultation to discuss your symptoms, treatment objectives, and the professional's approach to treatment. This encounter is an opportunity to assess compatibility and familiarity with the provider.
- Insurance and Costs: Verify insurance coverage for mental health services and inquire about the costs of treatment.

Many professionals offer sliding scale fees based on income, and some community health centers provide low-cost services.

- Commitment to Treatment: Engage actively in the treatment procedure. Attend sessions routinely, complete designated tasks or exercises, and communicate openly with your therapist or counselor.

**Integrating Professional Help with Support Systems**

Combining professional assistance with support group participation can provide a comprehensive support network:

- Holistic Approach: Utilize the strengths of both professional and peer support. Professional assistance can offer structured treatment and specialized interventions, while support groups provide community, empathy, and shared experiences.
- Consistent Communication: Keep your healthcare provider informed about your participation in support groups. This can help ensure a coordinated approach to your treatment and resolve any overlapping concerns or strategies.

# Chapter 8: Preventive Measures and Lifestyle Changes

Effective management of anxiety involves not only addressing current symptoms but also instituting preventive measures and lifestyle adjustments to reduce future episodes. Stress management techniques play a crucial role in this proactive approach. This section examines daily practices to reduce tension and long-term strategies that can help maintain a balanced, anxiety-free life.

## 8.1 Stress Management Techniques

### Daily Practices to Reduce Stress

Incorporating stress-reducing practices into your daily regimen can considerably mitigate anxiety and promote overall well-being. Here are some techniques that can be readily integrated into ordinary life:

**1. Mindfulness Meditation**

Mindfulness meditation entails focusing on the present moment and monitoring your thoughts and feelings without judgment. This practice can help reduce tension by promoting a sense of calm and awareness.

**How to Practice:** Set aside 10-20 minutes each day to sit quietly and focus on your respiration. Notice the sensations of respiration and gradually bring your mind back whenever it wanders. Apps like Headspace and Calm offer guided mindfulness sessions to help you get started.

### 2. Deep Breathing Exercises

Deep breathing exercises can rapidly calm the nervous system and reduce stress. By focusing on your respiration, you can interrupt the body's tension response and induce relaxation.

**How to Practice:** Practice diaphragmatic breathing by inhaling profoundly through your nose, allowing your abdomen to rise, holding for a few seconds, and exhaling gently through your mouth. Repeat this for several minutes, particularly during stressful moments.

### 3. Physical Activity

Regular physical activity is a potent tension reliever. Exercise increases the production of endorphins, the body's natural mood enhancers, and helps reduce levels of the stress hormone cortisol.

**How to Practice:** Aim for at least 30 minutes of moderate exercise most days of the week. Activities like walking, jogging, cycling, yoga, and dancing can be both pleasurable and effective in reducing tension.

## 4. Progressive Muscle Relaxation

Progressive muscle relaxation (PMR) involves tensing and then relaxing various muscle groups in the body. This technique helps reduce physical tension and foster relaxation.

**How to Practice:** Start with your toes and work your way up to your cranium, tensing each muscle group for 5-10 seconds before gently releasing. Focus on the difference between stress and relaxation.

## 5. Journaling

Writing about your thoughts and emotions can provide a therapeutic outlet for tension. Journaling helps organize your thoughts, obtain insights, and release pent-up emotions.

**How to Practice:** Set aside time each day to write about your experiences, challenges, and things you are grateful for. Keeping a stress journal can help identify triggers and patterns, allowing you to develop coping strategies.

## 6. Time Management

Effective time management can reduce the tension associated with feeling overwhelmed by duties and responsibilities. Planning and prioritizing can create a sense of control and efficiency.

**How to Practice:** Use tools like calendars, planners, and to-do lists to organize your tasks. Prioritize activities based on importance and deadlines, and divide larger duties into smaller, manageable steps.

## 7. Social Connections

Maintaining strong social connections can provide emotional support and reduce tension. Sharing your sentiments with trusted peers or family members can offer relief and perspective.

**How to Practice:** Schedule regular social activities, whether it's a phone call, coffee with a friend, or participating in group activities. Building a support network can provide solace and encouragement during stressful situations.

Long-term Strategies

In addition to daily practices, implementing long-term strategies can create a sustainable approach to managing stress and preventing anxiety.

## 1. Healthy Lifestyle Choices

Adopting a healthful lifestyle supports overall well-being and resilience to stress. This includes sustaining a balanced diet, receiving regular exercise, and ensuring adequate sleep.

- Balanced Diet: Eating a diet rich in fruits, vegetables, whole cereals, lean proteins, and healthy lipids can support physical and mental health. Avoid excessive caffeine, sugar, and alcohol, which can exacerbate tension.
- Regular Exercise: Engage in regular physical activity to maintain fitness and mental clarity. Exercise not only reduces tension but also enhances mood and energy levels.
- Adequate Sleep: Aim for 7-9 hours of excellent sleep each night. Create a soothing twilight routine and maintain a consistent sleep schedule to support restorative rest.

## 2. Cognitive Behavioral Techniques

Cognitive Behavioral Therapy (CBT) techniques can help modify negative thought patterns and behaviors that contribute to stress. By altering the way you perceive and respond to stressors, you can reduce their impact.

- Thought Challenging: Identify negative or irrational beliefs and challenge them with evidence and alternative perspectives. Replace your negative beliefs with more balanced and realistic ones.

- Behavioral Activation: Engage in activities that bring pleasure and fulfillment. Scheduling pleasurable and meaningful activities can counteract stress and improve overall well-being.

## 3. Building Resilience

Building resilience involves developing the ability to acclimate to duress and adversity. Resilient individuals can recover more swiftly from setbacks and maintain a positive outlook.

- Self-Compassion: Practice self-compassion by treating yourself with tenderness and understanding during difficult circumstances. Acknowledge your struggles without self-judgment and offer yourself the same support you would give a friend.

- Positive Thinking: Cultivate a positive mindset by focusing on your strengths and achievements. Practice gratitude by routinely reflecting on things you are appreciative of, which can shift your perspective and reduce stress.

## 4. Professional Support

Seeking professional support can provide additional tools and strategies for managing stress. Therapists, counselors, and coaches can offer guidance and interventions tailored to your requirements.

- Therapy: Engage in individual or group therapy to explore stressors and develop coping mechanisms. Therapists can provide evidence-based remedies like CBT to address stress and anxiety.
- Coaching: Life coaches can help set objectives, devise action plans, and provide accountability for implementing stress management strategies.

**5. Mindfulness and Relaxation Practices**

Integrating mindfulness and relaxation practices into your lifestyle can establish a foundation for long-term stress management. Regular practice can enhance self-awareness and emotional regulation.

- Mindfulness Meditation: Develop a consistent mindfulness meditation practice to remain present and reduce reactivity to stress. Start with brief daily sessions and progressively increase the duration as you become more comfortable.
- Yoga and Tai Chi: Incorporate practices like yoga and Tai Chi, which incorporate physical movement, respiration control, and meditation. These practices promote relaxation, flexibility, and balance, contributing to overall tension reduction.

**6. Environmental Modifications**

Creating a supportive and stress-free environment can significantly impact your stress levels. Consider making adjustments to your physical and social environments to enhance your well-being.

- Decluttering: Maintain an orderly and organized living and working space. A clutter-free environment can reduce tension and enhance focus and productivity.
- Nature Exposure: Spend time in nature to benefit from its tranquil effects. Regular exposure to green spaces, parks, and natural landscapes can reduce tension and enhance mental health.

## 8.2 Healthy Sleep Habits

Adequate and quality sleep is fundamental to mental health and well-being. Sleep plays a critical role in modulating temperament, cognitive function, and overall physical health. This section emphasizes the significance of sleep and offers practical suggestions for improving sleep quality to support anxiety management.

# Importance of Sleep

Sleep is essential for several physiological and psychological processes that contribute to overall health. Poor sleep can exacerbate anxiety symptoms, impede cognitive function, and negatively impact physical health. Understanding the significance of sleep underscores the need for developing sound sleep habits.

## 1. Regulation of Mood

Adequate sleep is necessary for emotional regulation and resilience. During sleep, the brain processes emotions and consolidates memories, helping to stabilize mood and reduce emotional reactivity. Lack of sleep can contribute to increased irritability, heightened stress response, and exacerbation of anxiety symptoms.

## 2. Cognitive Function and Performance

Quality sleep enhances cognitive functions such as attention, memory, problem-solving, and decision-making. Sleep deprivation impairs these functions, leading to difficulties in concentration, decreased productivity, and impaired judgment, which can contribute to anxiety.

## 3. Physical Health

Sleep is vital for maintaining physical health. It supports the immune system, assists in tissue repair, and regulates numerous metabolic processes. Chronic sleep deprivation is associated with an increased risk of cardiovascular disease, obesity, diabetes, and impaired immune function.

## 4. Stress Response and Resilience

Sleep plays a critical function in modulating the body's stress response. During sleep, levels of stress hormones such as cortisol are reduced, allowing the body to recover and restore homeostasis. Consistent, quality sleep enhances the ability to manage stress and reduces the overall impact of stressors on the body.

# Tips for Better Sleep

Improving sleep quality involves adopting healthy sleep practices and creating a conducive sleep environment. Here are practical suggestions to enhance your sleep:

## 1. Establish a Consistent Sleep Schedule

Maintaining a regular sleep schedule helps regulate the body's internal rhythm, promoting improved sleep quality.

- Set a Bedtime and Wake Time: Go to bed and wake up at the same time every day, even on weekends. Consistency reinforces your body's sleep-wake cycle.
- Gradual Adjustments: If you need to alter your sleep schedule, make gradual adjustments of 15-30 minutes earlier or later each day until you reach your desired schedule.

## 2. Create a Relaxing Bedtime Routine

A tranquil pre-sleep routine signals your body that it is time to settle down and prepare for sleep.

- Relaxing Activities: Engage in relaxing activities such as reading, having a warm bath, listening to soothing music, or practicing mild yoga or meditation.
- Avoid Stimulants: Avoid caffeine, nicotine, and other stimulants at least four to six hours before bedtime, as they can interfere with your ability to fall slumber.

## 3. Optimize Your Sleep Environment

Creating a comfortable and conducive slumber environment can significantly enhance sleep quality.

- Comfortable Bedding: Ensure your mattress and comforters are comfortable and supportive. Choose bedding that keeps you comfortable throughout the night.

- Control Light and Noise: Keep your chamber dark, silent, and cool. Use blackout curtains, earplugs, or a white noise machine to minimize disruptions.
- Temperature Control: Maintain a comfortable room temperature, typically between 60-67 degrees Fahrenheit (15-19 degrees Celsius), which is optimal for sleep.

## 4. Limit Exposure to Screens Before Bed

The blue light produced by phones, tablets, computers, and TVs can interfere with the production of melatonin, a hormone that controls sleep.

- Screen-Free Time: Establish a screen-free period of at least one hour before nighttime. Engage in tasks that do not involve electronic gadgets.
- Blue Light Filters: If you must use electronic devices before bed, use blue light filters or settings to reduce blue light exposure.

## 5. Be Mindful of Food and Drink

What you consume and drink in the hours leading up to bedtime can affect your sleep.

- Light Evening dishes: Avoid large, heavy dishes within two to three hours of nighttime. Opt for a light refreshment if you are famished before bed.

- Limit Alcohol: While alcohol might help you fall asleep initially, it can disrupt your sleep cycle and reduce sleep quality. Limit booze intake, particularly in the evening.

**6. Get Regular Physical Activity**

Regular exercise can promote improved sleep, but timing matters.

Exercise Timing: Aim to conclude vigorous exercise at least three hours before nighttime. Moderate exercise earlier in the day can help you fall asleep more readily and enjoy deeper sleep.

**7. Manage Stress and Anxiety**

Techniques for managing tension and anxiety during the day can also enhance sleep quality at night.

- Stress Reduction: Practice stress-reducing techniques such as mindfulness, meditation, and deep breathing exercises to soothe the mind and body.
- Nighttime Routine: Incorporate tranquil activities into your nighttime routine to facilitate the transition to sleep.

8. Avoid Naps

While brief naps can be restorative, lengthy or irregular sleeping during the day can negatively impact nocturnal sleep.

Limit Naps: If you need to sleep, limit it to 20-30 minutes and avoid dozing late in the afternoon or evening.

## 9. Use Your Bed Only for Sleep and Intimacy

Associating your bed with sleep can strengthen the connection between bed and relaxation.

Bed Association: Avoid using your bed for activities such as working, dining, or viewing TV. Reserve the bed for sleep and intimacy to reinforce its association with rest.

## 10. Seek Professional Help if Needed

If you continue to experience sleep difficulties despite implementing these guidelines, consider seeking assistance from a healthcare professional.

- Sleep Disorders: Conditions such as insomnia, sleep apnea, and restless limb syndrome require professional diagnosis and treatment.
- Therapy: Cognitive Behavioral Therapy for Insomnia (CBT-I) is an effective treatment for chronic sleep problems and can help address underlying issues contributing to sleep disturbances.

# 8.3 Balanced Life

## Work-life Balance

Achieving a healthy work-life balance is crucial for reducing tension and maintaining overall well-being. A balanced existence allows individuals to manage professional responsibilities while also dedicating time to personal interests, relationships, and self-care.

**1. Importance of Work-life Balance**

- Mental Health: A well-balanced existence reduces stress, prevents exhaustion, and promotes mental health. It enables individuals to recharge and maintain a positive outlook.
- Productivity: Balance enhances productivity and efficiency. When individuals are well-rested and less agitated, they perform better at work and in personal endeavors.
- Relationships: Balancing work and personal life promotes connections. Spending quality time with family and friends fosters emotional support and social connections.

**2. Strategies for Achieving Work-life Balance**

- Set Boundaries: Clarify the boundaries between work and private life. Avoid working during personal time and designate specific hours for work-related duties.

- Prioritize Tasks: Identify and prioritize projects based on priority and timeframes. Focus on high-priority work first and delegate or delay less vital chores.

- Learn to Say No: Politely decline additional work or commitments that can lead to overextension. Setting limits helps prevent exhaustion and maintains equilibrium.

- Take Breaks: Schedule regular pauses throughout the workday to unwind and recharge. Short pauses enhance focus and productivity.

- Flexible Work Arrangements: If feasible, negotiate flexible work hours or remote work options to better manage personal and professional responsibilities.

## 3. Integrating Self-Care

- Physical Health: Prioritize physical health through regular exercise, nutritious nutrition, and adequate sleep. Physical well-being directly impacts mental health.

- Mental Health: Engage in activities that promote relaxation and mental health, such as meditation, pursuits, and socializing with loved ones.

- Recreation and Leisure: Dedicate time to recreational activities and pastimes that bring pleasure and fulfillment. Leisure activities provide a mental respite and enhance overall well-being.

## Time Management

Effective time management is integral to attaining a balanced existence. By organizing and prioritizing tasks, individuals can reduce tension and increase productivity, leading to a more harmonious lifestyle.

### 1. Importance of Time Management

- Reduced tension: Effective time management prevents last-minute rushes and reduces tension associated with missed deadlines or unresolved tasks.
- Increased Productivity: Prioritizing and organizing tasks leads to increased efficiency and better use of time.
- Work-life Balance: Good time management allows individuals to allocate adequate time for work, personal life, and self-care, promoting balance and well-being.

### 2. Time Management Techniques

- Goal Setting: Set clear, achievable objectives for both short-term and long-term duties. Break huge ambitions into smaller, doable tasks.

- Prioritization: Use tools such as the Eisenhower Matrix to categorize tasks based on urgency and significance. Focus on high-priority duties first.
- Planning and Scheduling: Plan your day, week, or month. Use calendars, planners, and digital tools to schedule tasks and set reminders.
- Time Blocking: Allocate specific blocks of time for various duties or activities. Time restriction helps sustain focus and prevents multitasking.
- Avoid Procrastination: Identify and address the causes of procrastination. Break tasks into smaller stages, set deadlines, and use techniques such as the Pomodoro Technique to maintain focus.

## 3. Tools and Resources for Time Management

- Digital Tools: Utilize digital tools and applications like Trello, Asana, or Microsoft To-Do for task management and organization.
- Calendars and Planners: Use physical or digital calendars and planners to schedule tasks and monitor deadlines.
- Productivity Techniques: Explore productivity techniques such as the Getting Things Done (GTD) method, Bullet Journaling, or the Pomodoro Technique to enhance time management.

## 4. Continuous Improvement

- evaluate and Adjust: Regularly evaluate your time management strategies and make adjustments as required. Reflect on what works and what doesn't, and be open to attempting new approaches.
- Seek Feedback: Ask for feedback from colleagues, acquaintances, or family members on your time management practices. Constructive feedback can provide new insights and enhance efficiency.
- Education and Training: Invest in time management training or courses to acquire new skills and techniques. Continuous learning can enhance productivity and balance.

# Chapter 9: Dealing with Anxiety Triggers

Effectively managing anxiety involves recognizing and resolving the specific stimuli that precipitate anxious thoughts and reactions. Understanding these triggers allows individuals to develop tailored strategies to mitigate their impact. This section examines methods for identifying common and personal anxiety triggers, including the use of a trigger diary.

# 9.1 Identifying Triggers

## Common Triggers

Anxiety triggers are stimuli or situations that provoke anxiety. These can vary considerably among individuals, but certain stimuli are commonly reported. Recognizing these common triggers can provide a foundation for identifying and managing personal triggers.

### 1. Stressful Life Events

- Job Changes or Loss: Transitions such as beginning a new job, losing employment, or undergoing significant changes in job responsibilities can provoke anxiety.
- Relationship Issues: Conflicts, breakups, or changes in relationship dynamics with family, colleagues, or partners can induce anxiety.
- Financial Strain: Concerns about finances, debt, or economic instability often serve as significant anxiety triggers.
- Health Concerns: Personal health issues or the illness of a loved one can contribute to heightened anxiety, particularly if the condition is chronic or severe.

## 2. Environmental Factors

- Crowded or Noisy Environments: Being in crowded or noisy spaces can overwhelm the senses and induce anxiety.
- Public Speaking: Speaking in front of an audience is a common source of anxiety for many individuals.
- Social Situations: Interacting in social settings, specifically unfamiliar ones, can provoke anxiety, particularly in those with social anxiety disorder.
- Unfamiliar or Unpredictable Situations: Facing novel or unpredictable scenarios can lead to feelings of uncertainty and apprehension.

## 3. Psychological Factors

- Perfectionism: High personal standards and dread of failure can induce persistent anxiety.
- Negative Reasoning Patterns: Pessimistic or catastrophic reasoning can exacerbate anxiety symptoms.
- Trauma and PTSD: Past traumatic experiences can contribute to anxiety triggers related to recollections of the trauma.

## 4. Physical Factors

- Substance Use: Consumption of caffeine, alcohol, or recreational substances can provoke or worsen anxiety symptoms.

- Sleep Deprivation: Lack of adequate sleep can heighten anxiety and decrease the ability to manage stress.
- Poor Nutrition: An imbalanced diet lacking essential nutrients can negatively affect mood and anxiety levels.

# Personal Trigger Diary

A personal trigger diary is an effective instrument for identifying and comprehending individual anxiety triggers. By systematically recording instances of anxiety, individuals can detect patterns and gain insights into their specific triggers.

## 1. Purpose of a Trigger Diary

Keeping a trigger diary assists in:

- Identifying Patterns: Recognizing recurring situations or stimuli that consistently provoke apprehension.
- Understanding Reactions: Analyzing emotional and physical responses to distinct stimuli.
- Developing Coping Strategies: Creating personalized strategies to manage and mitigate the impact of identified triggers.

## 2. How to Maintain a Trigger Diary

- Format: Choose a format that suits your preference, whether a physical notebook, digital document, or a dedicated app. Ensure it is readily accessible for regular use.
- Details to Include: For each entry, record the following details:
- Date and Time: Note the specific date and time when the anxiety episode occurred.
- circumstance or incident: Describe the circumstance or incident leading up to the anxiety. Include as many specifics as feasible.
- Emotional Response: Detail the emotions experienced, such as dread, panic, sorrow, or frustration.
- Physical Symptoms: Record any physical symptoms, such as increased heart rate, perspiration, trembling, or vertigo.
- Thought Patterns: Note any negative or irrational thoughts that accompany the anxiety.
- Coping Strategies Used: Document the strategies employed to manage the anxiety and their effectiveness.

**3. Analyzing the Trigger Diary**

Regularly review and analyze your trigger diary to identify patterns and develop a deeper understanding of your anxiety triggers.

- Identify Common Themes: Look for recurring themes or situations that consistently provoke anxiety. These may include specific environments, individuals, or categories of events.

- Evaluate Responses: Assess your emotional and physical responses to distinct stimuli. Understanding these reactions can assist in developing targeted coping strategies.

- Refine Coping Strategies: Based on your observations, refine and modify your coping strategies. Identify which techniques are most effective for specific triggers and incorporate them into your anxiety management plan.

**4. Using Insights to Manage Triggers**

- Preparation and Planning: Use the insights obtained from your trigger diary to anticipate and prepare for anxiety-provoking situations. Develop a plan for managing these scenarios effectively.

- Stress Reduction Techniques: Incorporate stress reduction techniques, such as mindfulness, deep breathing, and progressive muscle relaxation, to mitigate the impact of triggers.

- Therapeutic Support: Consider discussing your trigger diary with a therapist or counselor. They can provide professional insights and help develop more effective coping mechanisms.

## 9.2 Coping Mechanisms

Coping mechanisms are essential tools for managing anxiety provoked by specific situations or stimuli. These mechanisms can be categorized into strategies for immediate response and long-term adaptations, both of which play crucial roles in maintaining mental well-being.

## Strategies for Immediate Response

Immediate response strategies are techniques employed at the moment to rapidly alleviate anxiety and prevent escalation. These methods can help regain control and soothe the mind and body during acute episodes of anxiety.

### 1. Breathing Exercises

Breathing exercises are highly effective in regulating the nervous system and reducing anxiety symptoms.

- **Deep Breathing:** Practice diaphragmatic breathing by inhaling slowly through your nostril, allowing your abdomen to rise, holding your breath for a few seconds, and exhaling slowly through your mouth. Repeat this cycle for several minutes to induce relaxation.
- **Box Breathing:** Inhale for four seconds, hold the breath, exhale, and hold the breath out for four seconds. This structured breathing pattern helps stabilize the heart rate and soothe the mind.

## 2. Grounding Techniques

Grounding techniques help redirect focus from apprehensive thoughts to the present moment, reducing the intensity of anxiety.

- 5-4-3-2-1 Technique: Identify five things you can see, four things you can touch, three things you can hear, two things you can smell, and one item you can taste. This sensory practice helps anchor you in the present moment.
- Physical Grounding: Carry a small object with a distinct texture, such as a polished stone or a fidget device. Focus on the sensations of the object to distract from anxiety.

## 3. Progressive Muscle Relaxation (PMR)

PMR involves tensing and then relaxing various muscle groups to reduce physical tension and promote relaxation.

Practice: Start with your toes and work your way up to your cranium, tensing each muscle group for 5-10 seconds before gently releasing. Focus on the contrast between tension and relaxation to relieve stress.

## 4. Visualization

Visualization techniques involve envisioning a tranquil and calming scene to reduce anxiety.

Guided Imagery: Close your eyes and visualize a serene place, such as a beach, forest, or mountain. Engage all your senses in the imagery, envisioning the sights, sounds, scents, and sensations of the place to promote relaxation.

**5. Positive Affirmations**

Positive affirmations are statements that reinforce self-worth and confidence, countering negative beliefs.

Practice: Repeat affirmations such as "I am calm and in control," "This feeling will pass," or "I am capable of handling this situation." Regular use of affirmations can help alter your perspective and reduce anxiety.

**Long-term Adaptations**

Long-term adaptations involve developing enduring routines and strategies that build resilience and reduce the overall impact of anxiety triggers. These approaches focus on establishing a balanced and healthful lifestyle to support long-term mental well-being.

**1. Cognitive Behavioral Therapy (CBT)**

CBT is an evidence-based therapeutic approach that helps modify negative thought patterns and behaviors contributing to anxiety.

- Thought Challenging: Identify irrational or negative beliefs and challenge them with evidence and alternative perspectives. Replace these notions with more balanced and realistic ones.
- Behavioral Activation: Engage in activities that bring pleasure and fulfillment. Scheduling pleasurable and meaningful activities can counteract stress and improve overall well-being.

## 2. Mindfulness and Meditation

- Mindfulness and meditation practices enhance self-awareness and emotional modulation, promoting long-term resilience to anxiety.
- Mindfulness Meditation: Develop a consistent mindfulness meditation practice to remain present and reduce reactivity to stress. Start with brief daily sessions and progressively increase the duration as you become more comfortable.
- Mindful Activities: Incorporate mindfulness into daily activities, such as mindful dining, walking, or breathing exercises, to maintain a tranquil and centered perspective.

## 3. Healthy Lifestyle Choices

Adopting a healthful lifestyle supports overall well-being and resilience to stress.

- Balanced Diet: Eat a diet rich in fruits, vegetables, whole cereals, lean proteins, and healthy fats. Avoid excessive caffeine, sugar, and booze, which can worsen anxiety.
- Regular Exercise: Engage in regular physical activity to maintain fitness and mental clarity. Exercise not only reduces tension but also enhances mood and energy levels.
- Adequate Sleep: Aim for 7-9 hours of excellent sleep each night. Create a soothing twilight routine and maintain a consistent sleep schedule to support restorative rest.

## 4. Building a Support Network

A robust support network provides emotional support and practical assistance, helping to manage anxiety more effectively.

- Social Connections: Maintain robust relationships with family, peers, and colleagues. Engage in social activities and seek support from trusted individuals when required.
- Support Groups: Join support groups, either in-person or online, to communicate with others who share similar experiences and challenges. Sharing and receiving support can promote a sense of community and reduce feelings of isolation.

## 5. Stress Management Techniques

Incorporating stress management techniques into daily life can help reduce the overall impact of anxiety triggers.

- Time Management: Plan and organize your tasks to prevent overwhelm. Use tools such as calendars, planners, and to-do lists to manage your time effectively.
- Relaxation Techniques: Practice relaxation techniques such as deep breathing, progressive muscle relaxation, and visualization regularly to reduce tension and promote relaxation.
- pursuits and Interests: Engage in pursuits and activities that bring pleasure and relaxation. Pursuing interests can provide a mental respite and enhance overall well-being.

## 6. Professional Support

Seeking professional support can provide additional tools and strategies for managing anxiety.

- Therapy: Engage in individual or group therapy to investigate anxiety triggers and develop coping mechanisms. Therapists can provide evidence-based remedies like CBT to address anxiety.
- Medication Management: Consult with a healthcare provider to discuss medication options if required. Medications can help manage symptoms and provide additional support when combined with other strategies.

By integrating these immediate response strategies and long-term adaptations into your life, you can effectively manage anxiety triggers and enhance your overall mental well-being. Developing a comprehensive approach tailored to your requirements can help you develop resilience, reduce the impact of anxiety, and lead a more balanced and fulfilling life.

# Conclusion

In our journey through understanding and managing anxiety, we have probed into its multifaceted nature and investigated a myriad of strategies for immediate relief and long-term resilience. This book has offered insights into identifying anxiety triggers, employing effective coping mechanisms, and embracing preventive measures and lifestyle adjustments to promote mental well-being.

**Key Takeaways**

Comprehensive Understanding: Recognizing the symptoms and categories of anxiety is crucial for effective management. Awareness empowers you to take control and seek appropriate interventions.

Immediate Relief: Techniques such as deep breathing, grounding exercises, and progressive muscle relaxation provide fast and effective relief during acute anxiety episodes, helping you regain composure and control.

Long-term Resilience: Adopting healthy lifestyle choices, maintaining a balanced diet, regular exercise, adequate sleep, and effective stress management techniques are fundamental for sustained mental health.

Cognitive and Behavioral Approaches: Cognitive Behavioral Therapy (CBT) and mindfulness practices help modify negative thought patterns and enhance emotional regulation, building resilience against anxiety.

Support Systems: Engaging with support groups and obtaining professional assistance are essential components of a robust support network, offering both practical advice and emotional encouragement.

**Next Steps**

Starting on this path requires fortitude, persistence, and self-compassion. Begin by incorporating one or two techniques that resonate with you, progressively expanding your repertoire as you gain confidence and experience. Seek support from loved ones and professionals, and continuously monitor your progress, celebrating minor victories along the road.

Remember, managing anxiety is a dynamic and ongoing process. Stay informed, remain open to new strategies, and continue learning to refine your approach. With dedication and support, you can attain lasting relief and lead a balanced, fulfilling existence.

**Resources for Further Reading**

To continue your journey, explore additional resources such as "The Anxiety and Phobia Workbook" by Edmund J. Bourne, "Feeling Good: The New Mood Therapy" by David D. Burns, and online platforms like the Anxiety and Depression Association of America (ADAA) and the National Institute of Mental Health (NIMH). Utilize applications like Headspace, Calm, and Insight Timer for guided support and meditation.

By leveraging these resources and remaining committed to your mental health journey, you can build resilience, reduce anxiety, and achieve a more tranquil and balanced existence. Remember, you are not alone, and with the proper strategies and support, you can navigate the complexities of anxiety and thrive.